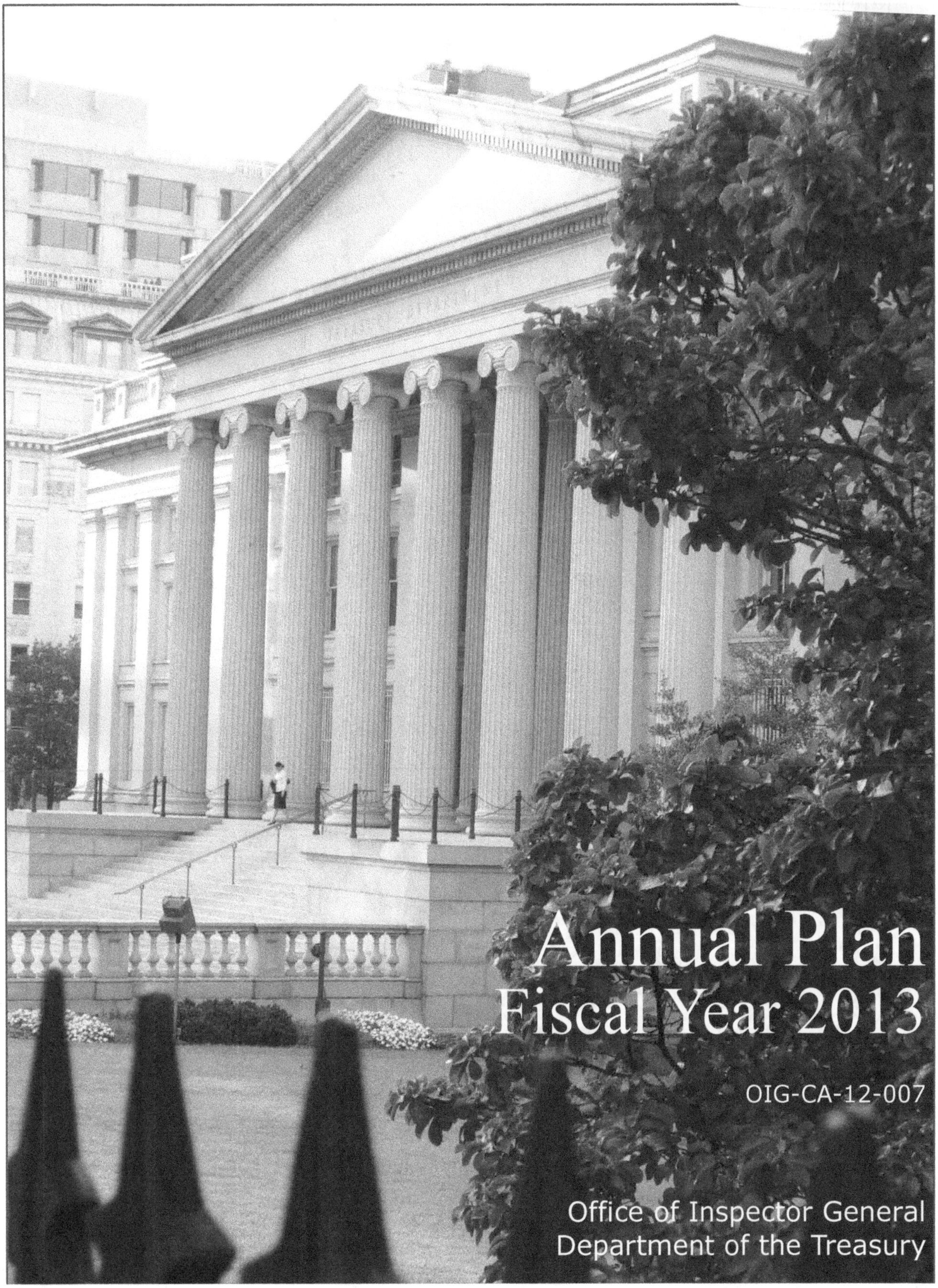

Annual Plan
Fiscal Year 2013

OIG-CA-12-007

Office of Inspector General
Department of the Treasury

Foreword

This annual plan outlines the fiscal year 2013 Department of the Treasury (Treasury) Office of Inspector General (OIG) audit and investigative priorities, which focus on the Department's major initiatives and challenges. The plan also takes into consideration the Treasury OIG's *Strategic Plan Fiscal Years 2011-2015*.

We have prioritized our resources to provide effective oversight for the most significant and highest risk Treasury programs and operations under our jurisdiction. For fiscal year 2013, our highest priorities are oversight efforts related to (1) the Dodd-Frank Wall Street Reform and Consumer Protection Act, (2) the Small Business Jobs Act of 2010, (3) the Bank Secrecy Act and USA PATRIOT Act of 2001, (4) the Housing and Economic Recovery Act of 2008, and (5) the Resources and Ecosystems Sustainability, Tourist Opportunities, and Revived Economies of the Gulf Coast States Act of 2012.

Other areas of emphasis for fiscal year 2013 include mandated audits as required by the Government Management Reform Act, the Federal Information Security Management Act, the Federal Deposit Insurance Act, and the Improper Payments Elimination and Recovery Act, among others. This plan also includes various Congressional directives, including reviews related to the Financial Crimes Enforcement Network's Bank Secrecy Act information technology modernization program, the Department's plan to consolidate the Financial Management Service and the Bureau of the Public Debt, as well as recent concerns with expenditures for travel, conferences, and awards.

In October 2012, the Department plans to consolidate the Bureau of the Public Debt (BPD) and the Financial Management Service (FMS) and to re-designate the two bureaus as the Bureau of the Fiscal Service. In this Annual Plan, we use Bureau of the Fiscal Service, or BFS, when referring to programs and activities of BPD and FMS.

Based on our assessment of the Department, the projects described in this plan address those areas of known and emerging risks and vulnerabilities. As before, we encourage Department and bureau management to use this plan to identify areas for self-assessment and to take corrective measures when vulnerabilities and control weaknesses are identified.

September 2012

Contents

Overview

Mission Statement

The Department of the Treasury (Treasury) Office of Inspector General (OIG) conducts independent and objective audits and investigations to promote integrity, efficiency, and effectiveness in Treasury's programs and operations.

Background

In 1989, the Secretary of the Treasury established OIG in accordance with the 1988 amendments to the Inspector General Act. As set forth in the act, we

- conduct and supervise audits and investigations of Treasury programs and operations except for the Internal Revenue Service (IRS), which in under the jurisdictional oversight of the Treasury Inspector General for Tax Administration (TIGTA), and the Troubled Asset Relief Program (TARP) which is under the jurisdiction oversight of the Special Inspector General

- provide leadership and coordination of policies that (1) promote economy, efficiency, and effectiveness in Treasury programs and operations and (2) prevent and detect fraud and abuse in Treasury programs and operations

- keep the Secretary of the Treasury and Congress fully and currently informed about problems and deficiencies in Treasury programs and operations

Organizational Structure and Fiscal Resources

OIG is headed by an Inspector General who is appointed by the President with the advice and consent of the Senate. As shown below, OIG's organization is comprised of five offices; all report to the Inspector General and are headquartered in Washington, D.C. OIG also has an audit field office in Boston, Massachusetts.

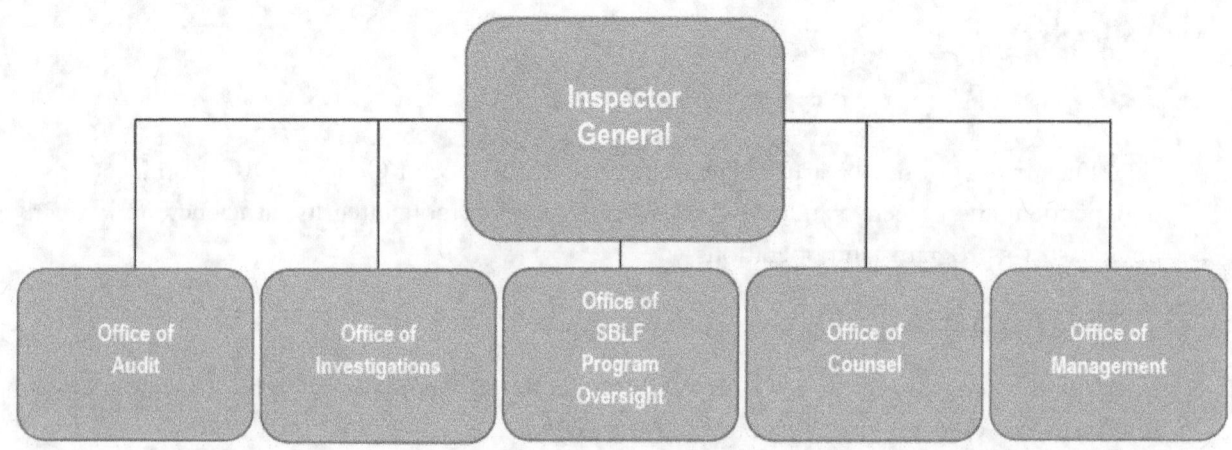

For fiscal year 2013, the President's budget request for direct appropriations for OIG is $28.6 million. The Office of Small Business Lending Fund Program Oversight is funded on a reimbursable basis by the Small Business Lending Fund (SBLF) and the State Small Business Credit Initiative (SSBCI) program offices. Estimated reimbursable funding for fiscal year 2013 is $4.1 million for SBLF oversight and $1.9 million for SSBCI oversight.

Performance Measures

OIG established performance measures for fiscal year 2013 for the Office of Audit, the Office of Investigations, and the Office of SBLF Program Oversight.

Office of Audit Performance Measures

- Complete 70 audit products
- Complete 100 percent of mandated audits by the required date
- Identify monetary benefits where appropriate

Office of Investigations Performance Measure

- Ensure 80 percent of investigative work product is referred for civil or criminal prosecution or administratively to a Treasury bureau for appropriate action

Office of SBLF Program Oversight Performance Measures

- Review 20 banks that have received SBLF funds
- Review 10 states allocated SSBCI funds
- Complete 100 percent of mandated SBLF audits by the required date

Fiscal Year 2013 Priorities

Audit Priorities

OIG established three audit priorities for fiscal year 2013.

Priority 1   Audit Products Mandated by Law

OIG allocates significant resources to meet mandated audit requirements, which include (1) audited financial statements and financial-related review work, (2) information security, (3) the Dodd-Frank Wall Street Reform and Consumer Protection Act (Dodd-Frank), (4) the American Recovery and Reinvestment Act (Recovery Act), (5) Treasury programs authorized by the Small Business Jobs Act, and (7) bank failures pursuant to requirements in the Federal Deposit Insurance Act. We also perform work in response to Congressional directives.

Priority 2   Work Requested by Treasury Management, Congress, or Other External Source

OIG typically receives two to three requests a year from Treasury management or Congress to perform specific work. The requested work is often already in our plan and requires only that we adjust the work schedule or scope. If the requested work is in a new area, we assess whether the work should be performed.

Priority 3   Self-Directed Work in Treasury's Highest-Risk Areas

With the resources available after we have completed mandated audit and requested work, we conduct audits to assess the Department's progress in addressing significant known and emerging risks and vulnerabilities. For fiscal year 2013, our self-directed work focuses on Treasury's responsibilities as they relate to the implementation of Dodd-Frank, anti-money laundering/terrorist financing programs, and Treasury's administration of programs authorized by the Resources and Ecosystems Sustainability, Tourist Opportunities, and Revived Economies of the Gulf Coast States Act of 2012 (Restore Act).

Our planned OIG staff resource utilization by these three priorities for fiscal year 2013 is shown in appendix A.

Treasury OIG Strategic Plan

OIG aligned its *Strategic Plan Fiscal Years 2011-2015* with Treasury's mission to maintain a strong economy and create economic and job opportunities by promoting conditions that enable economic growth and stability at home and abroad, strengthen national security by combating threats and protecting the integrity of the financial system, and manage the U.S. Government's finances and resources. The Treasury OIG mission is to promote the integrity, efficiency, and effectiveness of Treasury programs and operations under its jurisdictional oversight, which is accomplished through four strategic goals:

- Promote the integrity and effectiveness of Treasury programs and operations through audits and investigations

- Proactively support and strengthen the Department's ability to identify and manage challenges, both today and in the future

- Fully and currently inform stakeholders of Treasury OIG findings, recommendations, investigative results, and priorities related to Treasury programs and operations

- Enhance, support, and sustain a workforce and strengthen internal operations to achieve the Treasury OIG mission, vision, and strategic goals

While striving to achieve its strategic goals, OIG will demonstrate its values: excellence, integrity, respect, and innovation.

Relationship Between Treasury's Strategic Goals and Treasury OIG's Annual Plan Issue Areas

To accomplish Treasury's mission, the Department identified five strategic goals for fiscal years 2012 to 2015. To support Treasury's strategic goals, OIG will focus its work on nine issue areas.

The following table shows the relationship between four Treasury strategic goals and OIG's issue areas. The fifth strategic goal—pursue comprehensive tax and fiscal reform—principally impacts TIGTA, and is not addressed here.

Treasury Strategic Goal	OIG Issue Area(s)
Repair and reform the financial system and support recovery in the housing market	• Safety, soundness, and accessibility of financial services
Enhance U.S. competitiveness and promote international financial stability and balanced global growth	• Bill and coin manufacturing, marketing, and distribution operations • Domestic and international assistance programs • SBLF and SSBCI operations • Gulf Coast Restoration Trust Fund oversight
Protect our national security through targeted financial actions	• Terrorist financing, money laundering, and foreign assets control
Manage the government's finances in a fiscally responsible manner	• Treasury general management and infrastructure support • Government-wide financial services and debt management • Revenue collection and industry regulation

Office of Audit Initiatives

The Office of Audit plans to start 80 projects in fiscal year 2013 and to complete 58 projects started in prior years. Our ability to initiate new self-directed audits and complete those in progress will be affected by mandated work. We have identified 97 high-priority projects that must be deferred beyond 2013. Our in-progress and planned work and projects for future consideration are described in the Planned Projects by OIG Issue Area section of this document.

Investigative Priorities

OIG established four investigative priorities for fiscal year 2013.

Priority 1   Criminal and Serious Employee Misconduct

Our highest priority is investigating complaints involving alleged criminal and other serious misconduct by Treasury employees. OIG investigates allegations of the general crimes enumerated in Title 18 of the U.S. Code, other federal crimes, alleged violations of the Ethics in Government Act, and allegations of serious misconduct prohibited by the Standards of Ethical Conduct for Employees of the Executive Branch. Several Treasury bureaus and offices have additional rules and regulations relating to ethical standards for their own employees, and OIG also investigates complaints of alleged violations of these rules and regulations.

Priority 2   Fraud Involving Contracts, Grants, Guarantees, and Funds

We conduct investigations into allegations of fraud and other crimes involving Treasury contracts, grants, loan guarantees, and federal funds. Such allegations often involve contractors, entities, and individuals who are providing or seeking to provide goods or services to the Department. We receive complaints alleging criminal or other misconduct from employees, contractors, members of the public, and the Congress.

Priority 3   Financial Programs and Operations Crime

We conduct and supervise investigations relating to Treasury financial programs and operations. These programs and operations involve issuing licenses, providing benefits, and exercising oversight of U.S. financial institutions.

Priority 4   Threats Against Treasury Employees and Facilities

Our investigative efforts into threats against Treasury employees and facilities are critical in ensuring safety for the Department. These matters require prompt attention and coordination with federal, state, and local authorities in order to protect those involved.

Office of SBLF Program Oversight Initiatives

The Office of SBLF Program Oversight plans to start 4 SBLF audits and 10 SSBCI state reviews in fiscal year 2013. Our in-progress and planned work and projects for future consideration are described in the Planned Projects by OIG Issue Area section of this document.

Counsel Initiatives

The Office of Counsel supports OIG investigative, oversight, and audit activities by responding to requests for legal advice and reviewing and processing requests for the issuance of Inspector General subpoenas. In the area of disclosure, the office will provide timely responses to Freedom of Information Act and Privacy Act requests. It will carry out its litigation responsibilities in Merit Systems Protection Board and Equal Employment Opportunity Commission cases, as necessary. Based on experience, the Office of Counsel expects to process 40 initial Freedom of Information Act/Privacy Act requests and 3 appeals from those initial responses. In the area of electronic Freedom of Information Act, the office expects to review approximately 70 audit, evaluation, and oversight reports for posting on OIG's website. It will also

- provide ethics and standards of conduct training for all employees, and timely review all required confidential and public financial disclosure reports;

- review and update, as needed, Privacy Impact Assessments for all OIG operations and provide procedural review and training services as the OIG senior agency official for privacy;

- respond to *Giglio* requests, coordinate responses to document requests from Congress, and respond to discovery requests arising from litigation involving the Department and its bureaus;

- provide training on the Inspector General Act and other subjects in connection with new employee orientation and in-service training;

- review, as statutorily mandated, legislative and regulatory proposals and, where appropriate, coordinate comments; and

- review all allegations of misuse of the Treasury seal, name, and identification; and prepare cease and desist orders and penalty assessments, as needed, to carry out OIG's authority to enforce Title 31 of the U.S. Code, Section 333, Prohibition of misuse of Department of the Treasury names, symbols, etc.

Management Initiatives

The Office of Management provides OIG offices with a full range of administrative support, including budget and finance, facilities management, procurement, human resources, security, records management, asset management, and Information Technology (IT) services. The office is augmented by a working agreement with the Bureau of the Fiscal Service's (BFS) Administrative Resource Center for procurement, travel, budget execution, accounting, and human resource operations services.

During fiscal year 2013, the Office of Management will focus on providing timely, quality, and forward-thinking service to OIG customers. In addition, the office will continue to identify operational efficiencies to improve management support while identifying opportunities to reduce cost. In particular, it will look to reduce costs for travel, conferences, and fleet management in accordance with the Office of Management and Budget's (OMB) guidance, while ensuring that critical oversight and investigative activities continue.

The office's administrative services component will update and strengthen policies and procedures, manage the purchase card program, all purchase requests over the $3,000 threshold, and the travel program. It will also promote the use of public transportation and administer the public transit program, oversee security and safety initiatives, and implement OIG's long-range plan for space needs.

Security services will be a major focus during fiscal year 2013, as the Office of Management transitions from the Department's Office of Security Programs to the Administrative Resource Center for security clearance adjudication services. In addition, we plan to take additional steps in implementing, testing and training employees regarding Continuity of Operations planning.

The Office of Management's budget and finance component will work with the Administrative Resource Center to increase the timeliness of financial information and accuracy of budget projections, while adapting to the uncertainties of the federal budgeting process. The office will continue to provide for the efficient and effective reconciliation of financial transactions. It will also provide monitoring and oversight of billing and invoice approvals to ensure full compliance with the Prompt Pay Act, and the OMB's "Do Not Pay" list procedures, prepare and execute interagency agreements for services provided or rendered, respond to budget data calls, and act as liaison to the Administrative Resource Center for any system changes that impact OIG budgeting or accounting.

The office's human resources component will focus on the strategic management of the OIG workforce, working with hiring managers to recruit, hire, and retain employees within existing budget constraints and time-to-hire goals. It will focus on updating and communicating human resources policies and procedures and will initiate a newly-developed program for supervisory training. It will provide leadership in addressing goals set forth in the OIG's newly-developed Human Capital Plan and begin the process of transitioning to the new government-wide Senior Executive Service performance management system.

The office's IT component will continue to seek efficiencies through virtualization and service consolidation. Efforts continue to enhance the OIG's general support system; improve the ability of OIG employees to collaborate, either on-site or remotely; enhance the quality and choice of mobile communications; and ensure that all systems are fully maintained, operational, and in compliance with information security requirements.

Treasury's Management and Performance Challenges

In accordance with the Reports Consolidation Act of 2000, the Treasury Inspector General annually provides the Secretary of the Treasury with his perspective on the most serious management and performance challenges facing the Department. In a memorandum to Secretary Geithner dated October 24, 2011, Inspector General Thorson reported four management and performance challenges and one matter of concern. A synopsis of the matters included in that memorandum follow; the memorandum in its entirety, as well as prior years management and performance challenges memoranda, can be found at http://www.treasury.gov/about/organizational-structure/ig/Pages/Management-Challanges-Letter.aspx.

Transformation of Financial Regulation

Focuses on challenges with responsibilities of Treasury and the Secretary under Dodd-Frank

Management of Treasury's Authorities Intended to Support and Improve the Economy

Focuses on challenges with administering the broad authorities given to Treasury by the Congress to address the financial crisis under the Housing and Economic Recovery Act (HERA) and the Emergency Economic Stabilization Act enacted in 2008, the Recovery Act of 2009, and the Small Business Jobs Act of 2010

Anti-Money Laundering and Terrorist Financing/Bank Secrecy Act Enforcement

Focuses on the challenge facing Treasury to ensure criminals and terrorists do not use our financial networks to sustain their operations and/or launch attacks against the U.S.

Management of Capital Investments

Focuses on challenges with managing large capital investments, including the following ongoing IT investments: replacement telecommunications platform, common identity management system, data center consolidation, and the Financial Crimes Enforcement Network (FinCEN) Bank Secrecy Act (BSA) IT modernization program

Matter of Concern

This matter includes a discussion of increasing concern—information security, and the threat of cyber attacks

In October 2012, the Inspector General will update the management and performance challenges in a memorandum to the Secretary.

Planned Projects by OIG Issue Area

Treasury General Management and Infrastructure Support: Financial Management

Issue Area Discussion

Mandates

Financial audits are required for the Department and certain component entities pursuant to various statutes and other reporting requirements. The annual audit of Treasury's consolidated financial statements is performed pursuant to the Government Management Reform Act. OMB designated IRS as a Treasury component entity required to issue stand-alone audited financial statements under the act. Other Treasury component entities required to have stand-alone audited financial statements are the Bureau of Engraving and Printing (BEP), the Exchange Stabilization Fund, the Federal Financing Bank, the Mint, the Treasury Forfeiture Fund, the Office of D.C. Pensions, Community Development Financial Institutions (CDFI) Fund, the Office of the Comptroller of the Currency (OCC), and the Office of Financial Stability. The Alcohol and Tobacco Tax and Trade Bureau (TTB) and FinCEN financial statements are audited as a management initiative. In addition, certain accounts and activities of BFS that are material to the Department's financial statements are also audited.

Independent public accounting firms, under contract with OIG, audit the Department's consolidated financial statements and the financial statements of component entities, with the following exceptions: the Government Accountability Office (GAO) audits the IRS's and the Office of Financial Stability's financial statements and BFS's Schedule of Federal Debt, and OIG staff audit the Mint's Schedule of Custodial Deep Storage Gold and Silver Reserves and Treasury's Schedule of United States Gold Held by Federal Reserve Banks.

Program Responsibilities

Treasury also has responsibility for certain programs that will be reviewed as part of the audit of the fiscal year 2013 Department-wide financial statements including programs establish by (1) HERA, (2) the Emergency Economic Stabilization Act of 2008, (3) the Recovery Act, (4) the Small Business Jobs Act of 2010, and (5) the Terrorism Risk Insurance Extension Act of 2005 as reauthorized by the Terrorism Risk Insurance Reauthorization Act of 2007.

The purpose of the terrorism risk insurance program enacted under the terrorism risk insurance acts is to stabilize market disruptions that result from acts of terrorism. The program, which expires December 31, 2014, and has a cap on annual liability for insured losses of $100 billion, is in place to pay 85 percent of the insured losses arising from acts of terrorism above insurers' deductibles. Other programs established by the acts listed above are discussed in the Domestic and International Assistance Programs and SBLF and SSBCI Operations issue areas of this plan.

Working Capital Fund

The Department maintains the Working Capital Fund to centrally provide common administrative services across the Department and thereby achieve economies of scale and eliminate duplication of effort. These services are provided on a reimbursable basis to Treasury components at rates that recover the fund's operating expenses. For fiscal year 2011, Working Capital Fund expenses were approximately $125.1 million. Fund officials requested $57 million in funding for fiscal year 2013.

Improper Payments

The Improper Payments Elimination and Recovery Act of 2010 requires each agency to periodically review all programs and activities susceptible to significant improper payments. If a determination is made that a program is susceptible to significant improper payments, the agency must (1) estimate the amount of the improper payments, (2) report on actions that the agency is taking to reduce improper payments, (3) report on actions the agency is taking to recover improper payments, and (4) include this information in the accompanying materials to the annual financial statement. The act also requires agencies to conduct recovery audits of each program and activity that expends more than $1 million annually, if not prohibited by law and if it would be cost effective. The inspector general of each agency is required to annually determine if the agency is in compliance with the act.

Managerial Cost Accounting

Managerial cost accounting involves the accumulation and analysis of financial and nonfinancial data, resulting in the allocation of costs to organizational pursuits such as performance goals, programs, activities, and outputs, and should be a fundamental part of a financial performance management system. Both our office and GAO have reported the need for Treasury to implement managerial cost accounting more effectively. The Department developed a high-level managerial cost accounting implementation plan and revised its managerial cost accounting policy to improve managerial cost accounting practices throughout Treasury, promote consistency wherever possible, and address OIG and GAO concerns.

Known Weaknesses

The Department received an unqualified audit opinion on its fiscal year 2011 consolidated financial statements. The independent public accounting firm's audit report disclosed the following material weakness and significant deficiencies, and instance of noncompliance with laws and regulations exclusive of the Federal Financial Management Improvement Act.

- Material weakness—financial systems and reporting at IRS (repeat condition)
- Significant deficiencies—financial reporting practices at the Departmental level (repeat condition), financial accounting and reporting at the Office of Financial Stability (repeat condition), and information systems controls at Financial Management Services (FMS) (repeat condition)

- Instance of noncompliance with laws and regulations exclusive of the Federal Financial Management Improvement Act—noncompliance with Internal Revenue Code section 6325 related to untimely release of federal tax liens (repeat condition)

The auditor also reported that the Department's financial management systems did not substantially comply with the requirements of the Federal Financial Management Improvement Act related to federal financial management system requirements and applicable federal accounting standards.

In-Progress and Planned Fiscal Year 2013 Projects

Audits of Treasury Financial Statements and of Financial Statements or Schedules for Component Entities and Activities (In-Progress)

During fiscal year 2013, we will complete audit work for the fiscal year 2012 financial statements and schedules and begin audit work for the fiscal year 2013 financial statements and schedules. These audits will determine whether the financial statements and schedules are fairly presented in all material respects and will report on internal control, compliance with laws and regulations, and compliance with the Federal Financial Management Improvement Act. We will also award new contracts for the audited consolidated financial statements and several component statements as the prior contracts expire after the fiscal year 2012 audit.

Treasury's Compliance With the Improper Payments Elimination and Recovery Act of 2010

We will determine Treasury's compliance with the act. We plan to work with TIGTA in making an overall assessment of Treasury's compliance.

Office of D.C. Pensions' Quality Assurance Program Over Annuitant Benefit Payments

The Office of D.C. Pensions implements the Secretary's responsibilities under the Balanced Budget Act of 1997 to make timely and accurate federal benefit payments associated with the D.C. Retirement Programs for police officers, firefighters, teachers, and judges. These benefit payments totaled $537 million in 2011. During past financial statement audits, the auditor identified errors in annuitant payment amounts.

We plan to determine if the Office of D.C. Pensions' quality assurance program over annuitant payments is designed and operating effectively to detect mistakes in annuitant benefit payments processing.

Projects Under Consideration for Future Fiscal Years

Controls Over the Working Capital Fund

We plan to determine whether the Department established adequate controls over the Working Capital Fund. As part of the overall audit, we plan to determine whether: (1) fund activities and programs are appropriate for inclusion in the fund; (2) reconciliations between actual costs incurred by the fund and costs billed to participating Treasury bureaus exist, are timely prepared, and consistent; (3) costs charged by the fund are appropriate; (4) costs charged by the fund to specific bureaus are supported by appropriate documentation; and (5) assumptions, data, processes, and models used by the fund to estimate its annual costs are reasonable. We will coordinate our work as necessary with TIGTA.

Survey of XBRL

The eXtensible Business Reporting Language (XBRL) is a standards-based way to communicate and exchange business information between business systems. These communications capture reporting concepts as well as the relationships and other meanings commonly required in business reporting. It can offer cost savings, greater efficiency and improved accuracy, and reliability to those involved in supplying or using financial data.

We plan to determine whether XBRL can offer Treasury improved business capabilities for managing its programs and operations.

Implementation of Managerial Cost Accounting

We plan to assess whether Treasury implemented managerial cost accounting comprehensively and effectively.

Treasury General Management and Infrastructure Support: Information Security

Issue Area Discussion

External threats to Treasury's infrastructure and information include terrorists, criminals, and computer hackers. These malicious cyber threats have increased at an unprecedented rate and are becoming serious and difficult to detect given that hacking tools and malware are becoming more readily available and relatively easy to use. In addition, insider threats remain a serious concern. Because of the nature of Treasury's missions, ensuring the effectiveness of information security controls is paramount to prevent attacks and defend against malicious outsiders or insiders from doing the following:

- disrupting key Treasury functions (e.g., collection of revenues, issuing payments, managing the government's cash, producing coins and currency, preventing financial crimes)
- compromising classified or sensitive Treasury information
- obtaining or disclosing private citizen information
- destroying or altering information needed to accomplish Treasury's missions
- stealing valuable equipment or technology
- inappropriately using Treasury resources

In addition, the dynamic of cyberspace and technical innovations (e.g., e-commerce, social networking, and mobile devices) that provide greater convenience and accessibility to users also increase vulnerabilities to Treasury's information and resources. Because IT plays a crucial role in accomplishing all of Treasury's strategic objectives and activities, it is vital for Treasury to have an information security program that ensures the integrity of Treasury's information systems and the reliability and confidentiality of its data.

Mandates

The Federal Information Security Management Act (FISMA) requires OIG to issue an annual independent evaluation of the effectiveness of Treasury's non-IRS information security program and practices. TIGTA conducts the evaluation of IRS's information security program and practices. An independent public accountant, under contract with OIG, conducts the evaluation of Treasury's remaining unclassified security systems, incorporating TIGTA's evaluation into Treasury's overall results. We may from year-to-year exercise a contract option to conduct the unclassified security systems evaluation as an audit. In addition to the FISMA evaluation covering Treasury's unclassified systems, we conduct FISMA audits of Treasury's national security systems, including collateral systems and intelligence systems.

Based on the results of the fiscal year 2011 FISMA audit, we reported that Treasury's information security program for unclassified systems was in place and generally consistent with FISMA.

However, the program for Treasury's non-IRS unclassified systems was not fully effective in the areas of logical account management, security incident reporting, system security plan, audit log review, inventory of backup media, plans of action and milestones, vulnerability scanning and remediation, contingency planning and testing, backup controls, outdated and unsupported software, risk management program, personnel termination procedures, and system configuration management.

Program Responsibilities

Treasury was the first cabinet-level agency to move its public facing website into the "cloud", through the use of Amazon's EC2 (Elastic Compute) cloud hosting services for the stated purpose of improving the way citizens access Treasury data and information. This change is in part due to OMB's "Cloud First" policy for federal agencies, which requires that all agencies move at least one system to a hosted environment in 2011. Treasury.gov is the largest of multiple systems which Treasury hosts on public cloud, including FinancialStability.gov, MakingHomeAffordable.gov, SIGTARP.gov, and MyMoney.gov. All of these systems fall under the same contract and are housed in Amazon's EC2 cloud solution. With current trends in consolidation and hosting new systems on the cloud, auditing compliance of cloud-based systems with appropriate securities requirements will be essential.

In February 2010, OMB launched the Federal Data Center Consolidation Initiative to assist agencies in identifying their existing data center assets and to formulate consolidation plans that include a technical roadmap and consolidation targets. The initiative addresses the growth of data centers and assists agencies in leveraging best practices from the public and private sector to:

- promote use of green IT by reducing the overall energy and real estate footprint of government data centers;
- reduce cost of data center hardware, software, and operations;
- increase overall IT security posture of the government; and
- shift IT investments to more efficient computing platforms and technologies.

In December 2010, OMB announced an effort to close 800 data centers by fiscal year 2015, a move that is expected to save taxpayers more than $3 billion. Treasury is currently in the planning phase of an effort to reduce the number of data centers to 69 by fiscal year 2015.

The Treasury Data Center Consolidation Plan incorporated a move towards virtualization. Virtualization can be viewed as part of an overall trend in enterprise IT that allows an IT environment to manage itself and where users can pay for only the IT they use. The goal of virtualization is to centralize administrative tasks while improving scalability and overall hardware-resource utilization. With virtualization, several operating systems can run in parallel on a single central processing unit. This parallelism can reduce overhead costs and is thus an attractive method for federal agencies to realize cost savings. At the same time, full virtualization has security implications. In addition to adding layers of technology which can increase the security burden, combining many systems onto a single physical computer can cause a larger impact if a security compromise occurs. In some cases, virtualized environments are quite dynamic, which makes creating and maintaining the necessary security boundaries more complex.

In-Progress and Planned Fiscal Year 2013 Projects

FISMA Independent Review—Unclassified Systems (In-Progress)

We will determine whether Treasury's information security program and practices, as they relate to Treasury's unclassified security systems, are consistent with FISMA. We will also assess progress made in resolving previously reported FISMA weaknesses. During fiscal year 2013, we will complete audit work for fiscal year 2012 and begin work for fiscal year 2013.

FISMA Independent Audit—Collateral National Security Systems (In-Progress)

We will determine whether Treasury's information security program and practices, as they relate to collateral national security systems, are consistent with FISMA. We will also assess progress made in resolving previously reported FISMA weaknesses. During fiscal year 2013, we will complete audit work for fiscal year 2012 and begin audit work for fiscal year 2013.

FISMA Independent Audit for Fiscal Year 2013—Intelligence National Security Systems

We will determine whether Treasury's information security program and practices, as they relate to Treasury's intelligence national security systems, are consistent with FISMA. We will also assess progress made in resolving previously reported FISMA weaknesses.

Security Controls Over Treasury Information on the Public Cloud (In-Progress)

We plan to determine whether Treasury ensured effective security protection for its information on public cloud as required by federal policies and guidelines.

Disaster Recovery Exercises

We plan to determine whether Treasury and its components can recover operations in the event of a disaster. We will observe scheduled disaster recovery exercises on a selective basis. During fiscal year 2013, we plan to observe one exercise.

Network and System Security Assessments

We plan to determine whether effective security measures exist to detect and prevent unauthorized access to Treasury bureaus' networks and systems. To accomplish this objective, we plan to identify and exploit existing vulnerabilities in IT infrastructure to determine whether network-connected systems are (1) secure from unauthorized intrusion and misuse, (2) vulnerable to malicious security attacks, or (3) accessible through unauthorized or misconfigured paths (e.g., back doors into the network from the Internet or adjacent networks). In this regard, we perform a coordinated network security test by conducting automated and manual vulnerability assessments and exploitation. For fiscal year 2013, we plan to conduct audits at BFS and OCC.

Security Controls Over Virtual Servers Located in Treasury's Consolidated Data Centers

We plan to determine whether Treasury has proper controls for securing data on servers employing virtualization technology that are located in Treasury's consolidated data centers.

Security Controls Over Treasury's Industrial Control Systems

Industrial Control Systems in a manufacturing environment encompass several types of control systems, including supervisory control and data acquisition systems, distributed control systems, and other control system configurations.

We plan to determine whether BEP and the Mint maintain sufficient security controls to protect the control systems that operate their currency and coin manufacturing equipment.

Equipment Sanitation and Disposal

We plan to determine whether Treasury sanitizes and disposes of IT equipment, including digital copy machines and digital fax machines with hard drives, in accordance with federal regulations, and accounts for equipment before disposal.

Projects Under Consideration for Future Fiscal Years

HRConnect Security Controls

We plan to determine whether effective security controls over HRConnect are in place to protect sensitive information and prevent fraudulent activities.

Mobile Device Security

We plan to determine if Treasury implemented the appropriate security management practices and controls over mobile devices and supporting infrastructure.

Treasury's Government Security Operations Center Services

We plan to determine whether Treasury's Government Security Operations Center is providing an effective analysis of all security related events and data that traverse the Treasury-wide sensitive but unclassified communications network (TNet), as well as approved Internet access points across the Department.

Wireless Local Area Network Security

We plan to determine whether Treasury implemented appropriate security management practices and controls over wireless local area networks.

Remote Access Security

We plan to determine whether Treasury has proper security controls in place to protect Treasury's telework and remote access infrastructure as required by OMB and the National Institute of Standards and Technology.

Trusted Internet Connection Compliance

In November 2007, OMB issued Memorandum M-08-05, *Implementation of Trusted Internet Connections*, as an initiative to optimize individual network services into a common solution for the federal government. This common solution facilitates the reduction of external connections, including Internet points of presence, to a target of 50. Each agency was required to develop a comprehensive plan of action and milestones with a target completion date of June 2008.

We plan to determine whether Treasury's offices and bureaus have complied with OMB's Trusted Internet Connection initiative. We will also determine if the bureaus have connections to the Internet outside the two approved Trusted Internet Connections, and if they do, we will determine how they mitigate vulnerabilities associated with that access.

Enterprise Patch Management

We plan to determine whether Treasury bureaus have an effective patch management program to ensure timely and secure installation of software patches.

Continuous Monitoring and Risk Management

We plan to determine if Treasury has an effective continuous monitoring and risk management framework that meets current federal standards and guidelines.

Supply Chain Security

We plan to determine whether Treasury effectively managed supply chain risks for products and services that are contracted out.

Software License Management

We plan to determine whether Treasury is effectively tracking software licenses, including how and where the software is deployed.

Security of Treasury's Data on Websites Hosted by Third-Parties

We plan to determine whether Treasury ensures proper protections for its websites hosted by third-parties.

Treasury's Management of Large Scale IT Programs

As part of the Administration's initiative for IT reform in the areas of operational efficiency and large-scale IT program management, the U.S. Chief Information Officer issued the 25-point implementation plan to reform IT management on December 9, 2010.

We plan to determine whether Treasury effectively implemented OMB's reform initiative for managing large scale IT programs using a modular development approach.

Security Assessment of Treasury's National Security Systems

We plan to determine whether sufficient protections exist to prevent intrusions into Treasury's national security systems. To accomplish this objective, we will identify and exploit vulnerabilities that allow us to bypass IT system security controls that protect system confidentiality, integrity, and availability.

Privacy/Security Protection for Personally Identifiable Information

Section 522 of the Consolidated Appropriation Act of 2005 requires agency inspectors general to perform a periodic assessment of the implementation of this section of the act.

We plan to determine Treasury's compliance with Section 522 and OMB requirements for privacy and regulations for safeguarding against and responding to the breach of personally identifiable information.

Treasury General Management and Infrastructure Support: General Management

Issue Area Discussion

In addition to financial management and information security, the Treasury General Management and Infrastructure Support issue area encompasses other management activities to ensure that resources are used efficiently and effectively to carry out Treasury programs and operations. Examples of broad management activities that warrant audit coverage are discussed below.

Capital Investments

Sound business practices for the acquisition and maintenance of information systems (including hardware and software) are necessary to support Treasury's mission to manage resources effectively. Absent such practices, Treasury may

- develop or inadvertently acquire duplicate systems;

- pay higher prices for commercial off-the-shelf products by not obtaining volume discounts;

- develop systems that do not adequately address Treasury's needs or provide management with information needed to accomplish key missions;

- exceed projected or reasonable costs to develop, acquire, or maintain systems;

- acquire or develop systems that do not adequately secure and protect Treasury's classified, confidential, or sensitive information; or

- implement systems that do not readily integrate with existing systems.

Under the Clinger-Cohen Act of 1996, agencies are required to submit business plans for IT investments to OMB. In 2009, OMB instituted the IT Dashboard website where agencies report details of their IT investments. The site allows users to track the progress of IT projects over time. To identify IT projects at risk for excess costs or schedule delays, the cost and scheduling progress are rated against the agency's plan. For 2012, Treasury non-IRS bureaus reported 29 major IT investments. As of June 2012, the Treasury Chief Information Officer reported 3 IT projects as behind schedule—Electronic Federal Tax Payment System; Franchise Financial and Administrative Services; and Treasury Enterprise Identity, Credential and Access Management. The first two projects are also identified as expected to exceed projected costs. Projects identified as high-risk require special attention from the highest level of agency management but are not necessarily at risk of failure.

Past audits have indicated that the Department did not always effectively manage its capital investments (e.g., Treasury Building and Annex Repair and Restoration, the cancelled Treasury Communication Environment program, TNet, and BSA Direct). Certain capital investments, such as those for telecommunications, are funded through the Department's Working Capital Fund. Such projects do not receive the same scrutiny by OMB and Congress as those projects that are directly funded through the typical appropriations process.

Procurement

Procurements are a major Treasury activity. For example, between October 2011 and April 2012, Treasury non-IRS bureaus issued $2.4 billion in contract actions. Of that amount, $1.9 billion was issued by the Mint. Also, the use of government credit cards for micro purchases (generally goods and services under $3,000) is extensive, and strong control over this activity is essential to prevent abuse.

In 2011, Treasury transferred the majority of its Departmental Offices' contract activities to IRS. In 2013, the Department plans to transfer bureau procurement activities, except for manufacturing actions, to either BFS or IRS.

OIG is the Department's focal point for obtaining pre-award, costs incurred, and other contract audits requested by Treasury's Departmental Offices and the bureaus. These audits are typically performed by the Defense Contract Audit Agency and coordinated through our office.

Nonappropriated Activities

Three Treasury bureaus—BEP, the Mint, and OCC—do not receive appropriated funds; instead, they operate with revolving funds. BEP and the Mint assess charges to the FRB for manufactured goods, while OCC assesses fees to those banks under its supervision for regulatory activities. These three bureaus generally have greater latitude than Treasury's appropriated bureaus in how they finance their operations. Other revolving funds are administered by the Working Capital Fund and BFS's Administrative Resource Center.

Potential Integrity Risks

Potential integrity risks may result from the actions of external parties (contractors, terrorists, drug lords, and hackers) or internal personnel (disgruntled or unethical employees). Internal personnel, for example, can disrupt Treasury functions, violate laws, award contracts for less than best value, receive bribes or kickbacks, steal or reveal sensitive data, and cost the taxpayer money through the theft of materials and machinery, finished products, and mutilated products.

In-Progress and Planned Fiscal Year 2013 Projects

Corrective Action Verification (Ongoing)

Treasury and bureau management are responsible for implementing agreed-to audit recommendations made by OIG. Management records its planned corrective actions in response to audit recommendations and the completion of those actions in the Joint Audit Management Enterprise System (JAMES), a Treasury tracking system.

We plan to determine whether management has taken corrective action responsive to the intent of selected recommendations from prior OIG audit reports. In selecting recommendations for verification, we also consider recommendations that have been open more than a year to assess progress made toward implementing planned actions. Audit reports we plan to conduct verifications during fiscal year 2013 include, but are not limited to (1) *Consultation on Solyndra Loan Guarantee Was Rushed,* (OIG-12-048; Apr. 3, 2012) and (2) *Bill Manufacturing: Improved Planning and Production Oversight Over NexGen $100 Note Is Critical,* (OIG-12-038; Jan. 24, 2012).

Contract Audit Oversight Activities (Ongoing)

We plan to oversee and coordinate Defense Contract Audit Agency contract audit services requested by Treasury procurement officers.

CDFI Fund's Travel Expenditures (Ongoing)

We plan to determine whether CDFI Fund followed applicable law, regulations, policies, and procedures with respect to travel incurred in support of its programs as well as for conferences and outreach.

Treasury Procurement Activities (In-Progress)

We plan to determine whether selected Treasury bureaus and offices follow logical and prudent business practices that comply with laws and regulations and Treasury policies and procedures when procuring goods and services. We have audits in progress at BEP and OCC. During fiscal year 2013, we plan to initiate separate audits of the Office of Financial Research and BFS.

Classification of Treasury Information

The 9/11 Commission and others have observed that the over-classification of information interferes with accurate, actionable, and timely information sharing; increases the cost of information security; and needlessly limits stakeholder and public access to information. Over-classification of information causes considerable confusion regarding what information may be shared and with whom. It also negatively affects the dissemination of information within the federal government and others. The Reducing Over-Classification Act is intended to promote the proper classification of information. The act requires the inspector general of each department or agency, in conjunction with an officer or employee authorized to make original classifications and in consultation with the Information Security Oversight Office, to carry out no less than two evaluations of that department or agency's classification policies, procedures, rules, and regulations by September 30, 2016. The first such evaluation is required by September 30, 2013.

Consistent with the act, we will (1) determine whether applicable classification policies, procedures, rules, and regulations have been adopted, followed, and effectively administered within Treasury and (2) identify policies, procedures, rules, regulations, or management practices that may be contributing to persistent misclassification of material within Treasury.

Controls Over Travel, Conferences, and Employee Awards Programs

We plan to determine whether Treasury has effective procedures in place to ensure compliance with all applicable federal laws, regulations, and executive orders (E.O.) on travel, conferences, and employee awards programs. We are undertaking this work pursuant to Section 631 of the House Report 112-550.

Review of the Treasury Office of Security

We plan to determine whether (1) controls are implemented to ensure security clearance activities are conducted in a timely and appropriate manner and (2) security-related documents are secured.

Offices of Minority and Women Inclusion

We plan to determine whether the Department and OCC followed the requirements of Dodd-Frank in creating Offices of Minority and Women Inclusion.

Treasury Enterprise Identity, Credential and Access Management

In 2012, the Treasury Chief Information Officer identified Treasury's Enterprise Identity, Credential and Access Management system as having scheduling problems. Since 2007, Treasury spent approximately $178 million to implement the requirements of Homeland Security Presidential Directive 12 for a common identity standard. Treasury received funding of $69 million in 2012 and is requesting a budget of $66 million in 2013. The implementation is targeted for completion in 2018.

We plan to determine whether sound project management principles are being followed in carrying out the project.

Audit Resolution and Follow-Up

We plan to determine whether Treasury's audit follow-up system is effective to ensure that audit recommendations are promptly and properly acted upon and that progress on corrective actions is adequately monitored. This project is intended to complement our corrective action verifications on specific audits. As part of this audit, we plan to follow up on our recommendations in *General Management: Office of Management Needs to Improve Its Monitoring of the Department's Audit Follow-up Process*, (OIG-08-037; June 23, 2008).

Projects Under Consideration for Future Fiscal Years

Contractor Clearance and Background Investigation

We plan to determine whether controls are in place to ensure that Treasury's contractor personnel who have access to Treasury data and other information have current and appropriate security clearances and background investigations.

Treasury Secure Data Network Project Management

We plan to determine whether (1) the project business case for upgrading and enhancing the Treasury Secure Data Network, a classified communications system, is based on appropriate assumptions and cost/benefit estimates and (2) sound project management principles are followed in carrying out the project.

Management of the National Seized Property Contract

The Treasury Executive Office for Asset Forfeiture administers the Treasury Forfeiture Fund, the receipt account for the deposit of nontax forfeitures made by Treasury and certain other federal law enforcement agencies. In 2007, the Treasury Executive Office for Asset Forfeiture contracted with VSE Corporation for general property services in support of the Treasury Forfeiture Fund's mission. Since that time, the contract has had several protests filed that resulted in Treasury using bridge and letter contracts while a new solicitation is being planned.

We plan to determine whether the contracting actions and practices for the national seized property contract complied with policies, procedures, and guidelines established under the federal and Treasury acquisition requirements.

Employee Bonus Policies at Nonappropriated Bureaus

We plan to determine whether nonappropriated bureaus have (1) established policies for employee bonuses in accordance with applicable laws and regulations and (2) paid bonuses in compliance with applicable laws, regulations, and policy and procedures. Separate audits are planned at each nonappropriated bureau.

Controls Over Purchase and Travel Cards

Consistent with S. 300, the Government Charge Card Abuse Prevention Act of 2012[1], we plan to conduct periodic assessments of non-IRS Treasury purchase card and travel card programs and identify and analyze risks of illegal, improper, or erroneous purchases, travel charges, or payments in order to develop a plan for using such risk assessments to determine the scope, frequency, and number of periodic audits of purchase card or convenience check transactions and travel charge card transactions. We will also prepare joint reports with the Department as applicable under the act on violations or other actions related to Treasury purchase card and convenience check guidance or illegal, improper, or erroneous purchases with purchase cards or convenience checks.

Capital Planning and Investment Control Process

We plan to determine whether Treasury is appropriately managing its capital planning and investment process for IT projects.

PortfolioStat

The Administration's Campaign to Cut Waste directed agencies to seek opportunities to shift to commodity IT, leverage technology, procurement, and best practices government-wide; and build on existing investments. In October 2011, OMB launched the Shared First initiative aimed at reducing waste and duplication across the federal IT portfolio. In order to implement these initiatives, agencies

---

[1] S.300 was passed by the Congress and on September 25, 2012, was presented to the President. As of the publication of this annual plan, the bill was not yet public law.

are to review their respective IT investment portfolios to identify opportunities to consolidate the acquisition and management of commodity IT services, and increase the use of shared-service delivery models. To support this process, OMB issued Memorandum M-12-11, *Implementing PortfolioStat,* in March 2012 to require agency chief operating officers to annually lead an agency-wide IT portfolio review within their respective organization.

We plan to assess Treasury's implementation of PortfolioStat.

Treasury's Enterprise Architecture Program

We plan to determine whether Treasury complies with established federal guidance and Treasury's enterprise architecture policies and procedures, and to determine whether the Treasury aligned its strategic plans and individual business priorities within an appropriate enterprise architecture framework.

Resolution of Accountable Officer Irregularities

Accountable officers include certifying officers, disbursing officers, collecting officials, and other officers or employees who are responsible for or have custody of public funds. Treasury Directive 32-04, Settlement of Accounts and Relief of Accountable Officers, establishes the policy and procedures to settle irregularities (erroneous or improper payments) in the accounts of accountable officers. Requests for relief of accountable officers from liability for irregularities constituting a major loss must be referred to Treasury's Deputy Chief Financial Officer for resolution, except BFS accountable officers with government-wide fiscal responsibilities, who must refer to the Fiscal Assistant Secretary for resolution. The resolution of irregularities constituting a minor loss has been delegated to other Treasury officials.

We plan to determine whether irregularities in the accounts of Treasury accountable officers are resolved in accordance with Treasury Directive 32-04.

Treasury's Performance Data

The Government Performance and Results Act of 1993, as amended by the Government Performance and Results Modernization Act of 2010, requires the Department to establish performance measures for its programs. These performance measures are published annually in the Department's Annual Performance Report. Performance measure data is reported to the Department's Office of Performance and Budget by individual component entities.

We plan to review the Department's process to accumulate and report performance data and determine whether select performance data reported in the Annual Performance Report is appropriately supported.

Treasury's Reliance on Contractors

We plan to determine whether Treasury's programs demonstrate a balance between the use of contractors and full-time government employees, and determine if controls are in place to ensure contractors are not being used in 'inherently governmental' functions, or in functions that pose a potential conflict of interest or threat to Treasury's infrastructure.

Responsiveness to Freedom of Information Act Requests

We plan to determine whether the Department and non-IRS bureaus (1) have adequate systems to record, track, and timely complete Freedom of Information Act requests; (2) provide points of contact and monitoring systems to ensure that inquiries regarding existing requests have been properly addressed with the requesters; (3) revised procedures as a result of recent Supreme Court decisions; and (4) complied with the 1996 electronic Freedom of Information Act amendments.

Mandated Reports

We plan to determine whether Treasury has adequate monitoring controls in place to ensure the completion of presidentially and congressionally mandated reports. As part of this project, we will assess Treasury's progress to reduce, eliminate, or consolidate reports pursuant to the Government Performance and Results Modernization Act.

Treasury's Tribal Policy

The Office of Economic Policy is responsible for implementing E.O. 13175, *Consultation and Coordination with Indian Tribal Governments* (Nov. 2000) on behalf of Treasury. The order requires meaningful consultation and collaboration with tribal officials in the development of federal policies having tribal implications. The order is also meant to strengthen the U.S. relationship with tribal governments and reduce the imposition of unfunded mandates on Indian tribes. In 2009, the President issued memorandum directing department and agency heads to submit to OMB a detailed plan of action for carrying out the requirements of the E.O.

We plan to assess Treasury's implementation of a tribal policy and applicable guidance for carrying out policy to consult and collaborate with tribal governments and officials when developing federal legislation, regulation, and policy having tribal implications and resolving any issues and concerns raised by tribal officials.

Website Compliance With Section 508 of the Rehabilitation Act

Section 508 of the Rehabilitation Act of 1973, as amended, contains accessibility requirements for federal departments and agencies that develop, procure, maintain, or use electronic and IT. The purpose of Section 508 is to ensure that individuals with disabilities have access to and use of information and data in electronic or IT format—regardless of the type of medium of the technology—is comparable to the access to and use of the information and data by members of the public who do not have disabilities.

We plan to determine whether Treasury's website and its bureaus conform to the technical standards for web-based intranet and internet information of Section 508.

Telework Program Oversight

We plan to determine whether Treasury and non-IRS bureaus have adequate policies, procedures, and controls over employee telework.

Treasury's Management of Facilities

The federal government is the biggest property owner in the U.S. The President proposed a Civilian Property Realignment Board to sell or get rid of property it no longer needs. The Presidential Memorandum, "Disposing of Unneeded Real Estate," dated June 10, 2010, requires federal agencies to save no less than $3 billion by the end of fiscal year 2012. Treasury plans to save $11.7 million through real property cost savings for the fiscal year.

We plan to assess Treasury's effort to implement the President's Memorandum.

Physical Access Controls Over Treasury Facilities

We plan to determine whether sufficient protections exist to prevent unauthorized access into Treasury facilities.

Survey of Treasury's Human Resource Succession Planning

We plan to determine whether Treasury established human resource succession plans.

Terrorist Financing, Money Laundering, and Foreign Assets Control

Issue Area Discussion

Preventing terrorism, money laundering, and other criminal activity is a global effort. Treasury's role in this effort is to safeguard the U.S. financial system and protect it from illicit use. Treasury coordinates with other law enforcement agencies, intelligence agencies, foreign governments, and the private sector to add transparency to the financial system, which is designed to more easily detect those who would try to exploit the financial system for their own illicit purposes. Within Treasury, this effort is led by the Office of Terrorism and Financial Intelligence, which strives to safeguard the financial system against illicit use and other national security threats. The office oversees the Office of Terrorist Financing and Financial Crime, Office of Intelligence and Analysis, FinCEN, and the Office of Foreign Assets Control (OFAC). The Office of Terrorist Financing and Financial Crime manages the Office of Terrorism and Financial Intelligence policy and outreach. The Office of Intelligence and Analysis is responsible for intelligence functions, integrating the Treasury Department into the larger intelligence community, and providing support to Treasury leadership. FinCEN is responsible for Treasury's effort to enforce the BSA and the USA PATRIOT Act. OFAC administers laws that impose economic sanctions against hostile targets to further U.S. foreign policy and national security objectives.

BSA requires financial institutions to file Currency Transaction Reports for cash transactions exceeding $10,000 and Suspicious Activity Reports for transactions that are suspicious in nature. Law enforcement uses these reports to identify and guard against fraud, money laundering, terrorist financing, and other types of illicit finance. FinCEN focused its efforts in recent years on improving and increasing electronic filing of these reports. FinCEN is also in the process of implementing a BSA IT Modernization program that will reengineer BSA data architecture, update the infrastructure, implement more innovative web services and enhanced electronic filing, and provide analytical tools. FinCEN plans to complete BSA IT Modernization in 2014.

Title III of the USA PATRIOT Act requires each financial institution to establish an anti-money laundering program, extends the Suspicious Activity Report filing requirement to broker-dealers, requires financial institutions to establish procedures to verify the identities and addresses of customers seeking to open accounts, and requires FinCEN to maintain a highly secure network that allows financial institutions to file BSA reports electronically.

To better share information and improve coordination in ensuring that BSA is effectively implemented, FinCEN has a memorandum of understanding with the federal banking agencies—OCC, Federal Deposit Insurance Corporation (FDIC), the Board of Governors of the Federal Reserve System (FRB), and the National Credit Union Administration—and similar memoranda of understanding with IRS and most states and territories. FinCEN also has memoranda of understanding with the Securities and Exchange Commission and the Commodity Futures Trading Commission to enhance BSA compliance oversight in the nonbank financial sectors.

OFAC's authority to impose controls on transactions and to freeze foreign assets is derived from the President's constitutional and statutory wartime and national emergency powers. OFAC relies principally on authority under the Trading with the Enemy Act, International Emergency Economic Powers Act, and the United Nations Participation Act to prohibit or regulate commercial or financial transactions involving specific foreign countries, entities, or individuals. OFAC maintains a close working relationship with other federal agencies to ensure that these programs are implemented properly and enforced effectively. Like FinCEN, OFAC executed a memorandum of understanding with the federal banking agencies to share information and improve coordination.

In September 2010, FinCEN proposed a regulatory requirement for financial institutions to report cross-border electronic transmittals of funds. If implemented, such a requirement will greatly assist law enforcement in detecting transnational organized crime, multinational drug cartels, terrorist financing, and international tax evasion according to FinCEN. Implementation is dependent on completion of the BSA IT Modernization program. While we do not have any specific proposals related to this initiative in this annual plan, we will monitor the area for planning future work.

Areas of Concern

Terrorism, narcotics trafficking, human smuggling and trafficking, loan modification and foreclosure scams, mortgage fraud, health care fraud, and other organized criminal activity remain as high level concerns for the U.S. These activities all involve movement of funds and use of financial systems. Continued instability in the Middle East remains a significant challenge. In North America, increasing drug smuggling and violence related to drug cartels in Mexico have increased smuggling, crime, and violence along our Southern Border that may have also extended to our Northern Border. The financial crisis resulted in increased mortgage fraud and loan modification scams. Law enforcement continues to target organizations and individuals involved in defrauding the Medicare and Medicaid programs.

Over the last decade, the U.S. and others in the global community have required increased reporting and monitoring of financial institution transactions. In reaction to the activities largely occurring in the Middle East, including the nuclear development activities in Iran, the U.S. increased sanctions on transactions involving countries in these areas. Because terrorists and criminals are resourceful and cunning, they are reacting to the increase in financial institution monitoring by looking for ways of moving funds to support their illicit activity that more easily avoid detection. This includes, among other things, the use of electronic transactions (online and mobile) and prepaid instruments that make it increasingly difficult for financial institutions and law enforcement to detect illicit transactions, and the use of the nonbank financial sector where there is likely to be less monitoring and more opportunity to hide transactions, including money services businesses and informal value transfer systems.

Anti-money laundering/combating financing of terrorists remains a high priority. Our prior audits have revealed problems pertaining to the detection of BSA violations, the timely enforcement of BSA, Suspicious Activity Report data quality, BSA system development efforts, and administration of sanctions. Moreover, the universe of institutions required to comply with BSA requirements has grown as nonbank financial institutions participate in the program. The universe now includes the insurance industry and precious stones and metals dealers.

Potential Integrity Risks

Treasury efforts to support law enforcement in the fight against terrorist financing, money laundering, and other financial crimes are dependent on honest and complete reporting of currency transactions and suspicious financial activity. Potential integrity risks include (1) the failure by financial institutions to file required BSA reports, due to both poorly run programs and corrupt bank officials who are involved in the schemes; (2) filing of false or fraudulent BSA reports; (3) internal and external misuse or disclosure of sensitive BSA information contrary to law; (4) inappropriate handling or use of sensitive but unclassified, law enforcement–sensitive, or classified information; and (5) criminal violations of the foreign sanctions program.

In-Progress and Planned Fiscal Year 2013 Projects

FinCEN BSA IT Modernization Program (In-Progress)

Pursuant to a Congressional directive, we are conducting a series of audits to determine whether FinCEN is (1) meeting cost, schedule, and performance benchmarks for the BSA IT Modernization program, and (2) providing appropriate contractor oversight. During fiscal year 2012, we issued two reports under this directive. We will report on these objectives every 6 months until the system development is completed in 2014.

OFAC Libyan Sanctions Case Study (In-Progress)

The President issued E.O. 13566 on February 25, 2011, blocking property and prohibiting certain transactions related to Libya in order to protect Libyan state assets from misappropriation. This order was issued based on findings that Colonel Muammar Qadhafi, his government, and close associates, have taken extreme measures against the people of Libya, including using weapons of war, mercenaries, and wanton violence against unarmed civilians. By March 1, 2011, Treasury reported at least $30 billion in Government of Libya assets were frozen under the E.O. The reported amount of frozen Libyan assets increased to approximately $37 billion by September 2011. In an effort to return the frozen assets to the Libyan people, on September 1, 2011, OFAC released an initial $700 million in frozen assets to the Libyan Transitional National Council for fuel and civilian operating costs and to pay salaries in support of the Libyan people. Treasury announced that going forward; it would remain in close contact with the council for the release of additional assets. On December 16, 2011, the U.S. unfroze all Libyan government and Central Bank funds within U.S. jurisdiction, with limited exceptions. Only those assets in the U.S. of the Qadhafi family and former members of the former Qadhafi regime remain frozen.

We plan to perform a case study on OFAC's implementation and subsequent lifting of most of the sanctions against Libya. For the purpose of this project, we plan to (1) review OFAC's implementation of the Libyan sanctions program; (2) determine how frozen assets are identified, maintained, and accounted for; (3) review OFAC's subsequent and gradual release of frozen Libyan assets; and (4) determine how OFAC will identify and release all frozen assets to their rightful owners upon termination of the sanctions program.

OCC's BSA and USA PATRIOT Act Compliance Examinations and Enforcement Actions (In-Progress)

We plan to determine the effectiveness of OCC's programs to conduct supervisory activities and, when necessary, take enforcement actions to ensure that national banks have controls in place and provide the requisite notices to law enforcement to deter and detect money laundering, terrorist financing, and other related criminal acts. The scope of this review will include OCC's examination coverage of BSA compliance by former thrifts supervised by the former Office of Thrift Supervision (OTS), which were transferred to OCC in July 2011. Additionally, the scope of this review will include national bank trust departments and banks offering both private banking services and correspondent bank accounts (which make payments or handle transactions on behalf of a foreign bank).

Treasury Executive Office of Asset Forfeiture's Use of Treasury Forfeiture Fund Receipts to Support Law Enforcement (In-Progress)

We plan to determine whether the Treasury Executive Office of Asset Forfeiture has appropriate controls to (1) award and distribute funds to eligible law enforcement agencies in accordance with applicable laws, regulations, and policies; and (2) ensure that distributed receipts are used for intended purposes. As part of this work, we plan to determine whether selected state and local government agencies use Treasury forfeiture funds in accordance with Treasury guidelines.

FinCEN Civil Penalties for BSA Program Violations

We plan to determine FinCEN's process for assessing and collecting civil penalties when BSA violations occur.

FinCEN Implementation of USA PATRIOT Act Information-Sharing Procedures

The USA PATRIOT Act provides for the sharing of information between the government and financial institutions, and among financial institutions regarding individuals, entities, and organizations engaged in or reasonably suspected of engaging in terrorist acts or money laundering activities. In March 2005, FinCEN implemented a web-based secure communications system to expedite sharing of this information.

We plan to determine the extent to which information sharing is occurring among the government and financial institutions.

Impact of FinCEN's Rules on Financial Institutions Subject to the Comprehensive Iran Sanctions, Accountability, and Divestment Act

The Comprehensive Iran Sanctions, Accountability and Divestment Act of 2010 imposed sanctions aimed at persuading the Iranian government to end its illicit nuclear program. The financial sanctions prescribed by the act were designed to restrict or prohibit U.S. financial institutions from doing business with foreign institutions related to or conducting business with the government of Iran or its agents. Under the act, FinCEN was authorized to require U.S. banks to perform sanctions audits on foreign financial institutions with which they keep correspondent accounts to determine if those institutions are in compliance with requirements of the act. FinCEN issued the final rule on October 2011.

We plan to assess FinCEN's efforts to ensure financial institution compliance with the final rule.

Follow-up on a Classified Program

We plan to follow-up on the implementation of recommendations made in an audit report of a classified program.

OFAC's Management of the Specially Designated Nationals and Blocked Persons List

OFAC is responsible for enforcing economic and trade sanctions against targeted foreign countries, terrorists, and international narcotics traffickers. A major component to these sanctions is the Specially Designated Nationals and Blocked Persons list, which includes over 3,500 names of individuals, governments, and companies that serve as agents or representatives of countries with which U.S. businesses and citizens are prohibited from engaging in trade. In consultation with the Departments of State and Justice, OFAC relies on both public and classified data to list an entity on the list. Entities who wish to challenge OFAC's designation can apply to OFAC for delisting, and must credibly demonstrate they no longer engage in or plan to engage in the sanctioned activity, and that the circumstances resulting in the designation no longer apply. Over the last 3 years, OFAC reported that it removed about 1,500 entities from the list and expects to remove at least 600 more by the end of 2012. In a related development, in June 2012, OFAC announced it launched a new Specially Designated Nationals data system.

We plan to determine and assess OFAC's management controls over the process of listing and delisting individuals and entities from the Specially Designated Nationals and Blocked Persons list and assess the effectiveness of the new data system in helping OFAC manage this process.

Responsibilities of the Office of Intelligence and Analysis Under the Intelligence Authorization Act

The Intelligence Authorization Act for Fiscal Year 2004 established the Office of Intelligence and Analysis and assigned it responsibility for receiving, analyzing, collating, and disseminating foreign intelligence and foreign counterintelligence information related to Treasury operations.

We plan to assess the office's progress toward meeting its responsibilities.

OFAC's Resources Allocated to the Cuban Embargo

The Cuban Democracy Act, enacted in 1992, is intended to support democracy in Cuba by further restricting U.S. trade with the Cuban government and encouraging other countries to limit their trade. This law outlined specific measures either permitting or restricting U.S. activities with Cuba.

We plan to determine the degree to which OFAC's resources are used to administer Cuban sanctions activities.

Terrorist Finance Tracking Program

After the terrorist attacks on September 11, 2001, Treasury initiated the Terrorist Finance Tracking Program to identify, track, and pursue terrorists and their networks. During 2010, the U.S. and the European Union entered into a new agreement on the transfer and processing of data in the Terrorist Finance Tracking Program. As provided in the agreement, we will provide appropriate oversight of the program.

Projects Under Consideration for Future Fiscal Years

FinCEN Efforts to Identify Fraud

We plan to survey FinCEN's efforts in proactively identifying potential healthcare, mortgage, insurance, and other frauds; and in disseminating that information to law enforcement and regulatory agencies. The survey results will be used to determine whether more in-depth audit coverage of this area is warranted.

OFAC Civil Penalty Cases (Follow-Up)

OFAC enforces economic sanctions by issuing civil and criminal penalties. These penalties serve as a deterrent to acts that violate sanctions programs. Past audits have revealed that some civil and criminal cases have not been acted upon in a timely fashion allowing them to fall out of the statute of limitation term. If illegal acts go unpunished, this could result in more violations of foreign sanctions since there would be no consequence for not complying with these sanctions. In 2006, we reported that OFAC had allowed hundreds of enforcement cases to expire without issuing civil money penalties because of poor case management.

We plan to determine if OFAC has implemented effective case management processes for its civil and criminal penalty activities.

Examinations of Nonbank Financial Institutions for BSA Compliance

FinCEN has the responsibility for oversight of the BSA for nonbank financial institutions which do not have a federal functional regulator. FinCEN delegated examination authority for these institutions to IRS. In an effort to better leverage examination resources, FinCEN is looking also to coordinate with the states.

We plan to determine how FinCEN is ensuring that nonbank institutions are compliant with the BSA.

Financial Institution Filing of Reports to OFAC and FinCEN on Blocked Transactions

In December 2004, FinCEN advised institutions subject to BSA suspicious activity reporting that under certain circumstances reports filed with OFAC related to blocked transactions with designated terrorists, foreign terrorist organizations, and narcotics traffickers and trafficker kingpins would fulfill the requirement to file suspicious activity reports with FinCEN (i.e., a separate suspicious activity report to FinCEN on the same blocked transaction would no longer be required). However, if the institution has information not included on the blocking report filed with OFAC, a suspicious activity report containing that information must still be filed with FinCEN.

We plan to determine whether OFAC and FinCEN implemented controls to ensure that the information in reports filed with OFAC on blocked transactions is made available to law enforcement through FinCEN databases as appropriate.

Treasury's Guidance on Monitoring Electronic Money

Electronic money is also known as e-money, e-currency, electronic cash, electronic currency, digital money, digital cash, digital currency, or cyber currency. Typically, e-money involves the use of computer networks, the internet and digital stored value systems. Electronic funds transfer, direct deposit, digital gold currency, and virtual currency are all examples of electronic money.

Digital currencies provide a potential money laundering instrument because they facilitate international payments without the transmittal services of traditional financial institutions. "Identified" e-money contains information revealing the identity of the person who originally withdrew the money from the bank, and enables the bank to track the money as it moves through the economy. "Anonymous" e-money works just like real paper cash. Once anonymous, it is withdrawn from an account and can be spent or given away without leaving a transaction trail.

We plan to determine if Treasury provided timely guidance for agencies to monitor e-money products, and how Treasury is addressing the vulnerabilities to the financial system with the use of these products.

FinCEN Memorandum of Understanding With Financial Institution Regulators

FinCEN executed a memorandum of understanding with the four federal banking regulators (OCC, FDIC, FRB, and National Credit Union Administration) to better share information and improve coordination. The purpose of the memorandum of understanding is to help FinCEN fulfill its role as administrator and enforcer of economic sanctions and to help the regulators fulfill their roles as banking organization supervisors.

We plan to determine whether (1) FinCEN is receiving timely, complete, and reliable information in accordance with the memorandum of understanding and (2) the purpose of the memorandum of understanding, which was to enhance communication and coordination enabling financial institutions to identify, deter, and interdict terrorist financing and money laundering, is being achieved. We plan to address these objectives by conducting audit work at FinCEN and OCC.

OFAC Memorandum of Understanding With Financial Institution Regulators

OFAC executed a memorandum of understanding with the four federal banking regulators to better share information and improve coordination. The purpose of the memorandum of understanding is to help OFAC fulfill its role as administrator and enforcer of economic sanctions and to help the regulators fulfill their roles as banking organization supervisors.

We plan to determine (1) whether OFAC is receiving timely, complete, and reliable information under the April 2006 memorandum of understanding with the financial institution regulators and (2) if the memorandum of understanding is achieving its purpose of helping OFAC administer and enforce economic sanctions and assisting banking regulators in fulfilling their roles as banking organization supervisors. We plan to conduct audit work at OFAC and OCC.

Treasury's Compliance With Intelligence Reporting Requirements

E.O. 13462, *President's Intelligence Advisory Board and Intelligence Oversight Board,* as amended, requires Treasury to report intelligence gathering activities to the Intelligence Oversight Board and the President's Intelligence Advisory Board. These boards are responsible for keeping the President apprised of issues discovered through intelligence gathering activities throughout the federal government. Under E.O. 13462 and the *Criteria on Thresholds for Reporting Intelligence Oversight Matters and Instructions Relating to Formatting and Scheduling,* the Office of Intelligence and Analysis is responsible for submitting quarterly reports on intelligence activities that it has reason to believe may be unlawful or contrary to E.O. or Presidential directive to the Intelligence Oversight Board of the President's Intelligence Advisory Board and the Director of National Intelligence. This quarterly report also covers any matters considered "significant or highly sensitive" as defined under the criteria. The E.O. also requires Treasury to act on any recommendations made by the board and the Director of National Intelligence, including instructions to discontinue activities that may be unlawful or contrary to E.O.s or other Presidential directives.

We plan to determine if Treasury established effective policies and procedures in meeting the requirements of E.O. 13462, and is taking appropriate actions when directed to by the Intelligence Oversight Board or the Director of National Intelligence.

FinCEN Efforts to Assess Risks Associated With the Use of Prepaid Access Products

Law enforcement officials have expressed concern about the possible illicit use of prepaid access, either in the form of cards, electronic media, or other products. Prepaid access is defined as access to funds (or the future value of funds) that have been paid in advance and can be retrieved or transferred in the future through an electronic device or vehicle, such as a card, code, electronic serial number, mobile identification number, or personal identification number.

Prepaid access cards, for example, can be carried in wallets with credit cards, are often indistinguishable from credit cards, and can often be used anonymously, making them a potential vehicle for money launderers or terrorists. The most recent estimates available suggest that prepaid access cards are being increasingly used by Latin American and Canadian drug cartels to annually launder an estimated $50 billion to $100 billion from U.S. illegal drug sales across the border. In July 2011, FinCEN issued a final rule to clarify the definition of prepaid access and impose suspicious activity reporting, customer identification, and recordkeeping requirements on both providers and sellers of prepaid access, and registration requirements on sellers.

We plan to assess the implementation of FinCEN's guidance in the prepaid access final rule.

Office of Terrorist Financing and Financial Crimes Interagency Collaboration With the National Security Community

The Office of Terrorist Financing and Financial Crimes develops initiatives and deploys strategies to combat money laundering, terrorist financing, weapons of mass destruction proliferation, and other criminal and illicit activities, both domestically and abroad. This effort requires the Office of Terrorist Financing and Financial Crimes to work among the national security community, including the law enforcement, regulatory, policy, diplomatic and intelligence communities as well as with the private sector and foreign governments in order to identify and address threats to the international financial system of illicit finance.

We plan to assess the Office of Terrorist Financing and Financial Crimes' collaboration with the national security community, including the law enforcement, regulatory, policy, diplomatic and intelligence communities as well as with the private sector and foreign governments in order to identify and address threats to the international financial system of illicit finance.

Security Controls Over Forfeited Property

The Treasury Executive Office for Asset Forfeiture manages the Treasury Forfeiture Fund. Forfeited general property, vessels, aircraft, and vehicles are stored at warehouse locations across the U.S. and are managed by a contractor. The stored property is either sold, destroyed, or equitably shared with law enforcement agencies.

We plan to assess the security controls over forfeited property stored in contractor facilities.

Disposition of Forfeited Property

We plan to evaluate the Treasury Forfeiture Fund's controls over the disposition of forfeited property. In addition, we will determine whether the property contractor is disposing of property in compliance with the terms of the contract.

OFAC's Licensing Database System Upgrade

OFAC uses a document management system to store licensing data obtained from license applications and related correspondence. In 2012, OFAC completed a systems development effort to better manage licensing information. The goal of the project is to provide OFAC with an integrated, largely paperless database that would allow it to better collect and manage information, conduct analysis, and improve efficiency.

We plan to determine whether the upgrade to OFAC's licensing system is meeting the needs of OFAC's Licensing Division.

FinCEN's Oversight of BSA Examination and Enforcement for Nonbank Residential Mortgage Originators and Brokers

In February 2012, FinCEN issued final regulations requiring nonbank residential mortgage lenders and originators to establish anti-money laundering programs and file suspicious activity reports. FinCEN believes that the new regulations will help mitigate risks and minimize vulnerabilities that criminals have exploited in the nonbank residential mortgage sector. FinCEN is unsure of who will examine these institutions for BSA compliance, though IRS, state regulatory agencies, the Consumer Financial Protection Bureau, and the federal banking agencies could all be involved. Upon consideration of all the comments, FinCEN states that it will work with other relevant regulatory agencies in the development of consistent compliance examination processes.

We plan to evaluate FinCEN's strategy for establishing an examination and compliance program for nonbank mortgage originators and brokers.

Government-wide Financial Services and Debt Management

Issue Area Discussion

In October 2012, the Bureau of the Public Debt (BPD) and the Financial Management Service (FMS) are to begin consolidating operations, becoming BFS. Treasury expects the consolidation to improve the delivery of public service, reduce the footprint of the federal government, and manage administrative and IT costs. The consolidation is intended to allow BFS to take advantage of economies of scale, eliminate overlapping and duplicative functions, and reduce administrative overhead and support services costs. In addition, it will consolidate its payment centers from four to two in fiscal year 2014. Treasury estimates that BFS will have 65 fewer full-time equivalent employees in 2013 than 2012 and a smaller budget by $41 million. The consolidation is expected to be completed in fiscal year 2014.

Treasury, through BFS, borrows the money needed to operate the federal government, accounts for the resulting debt, and provides reimbursable support services to federal agencies. The goal of Treasury debt management is to achieve the lowest borrowing costs over time by committing to regular and predictable debt issuance. Treasury debt management decisions are made through deliberate and distinct processes utilizing new information as it becomes available.

The federal debt has two major components: Debt Held by the Public and Intragovernmental Holdings. Debt Held by the Public is the debt held by individuals, corporations, state or local governments, foreign governments, and other entities outside the U.S. government. Types of securities held by the public include Treasury Bills, Treasury Notes, Treasury Bonds, Treasury Inflation-Protected Securities, U.S. Savings Bonds, State and Local Government Series Securities, Foreign Series securities, and Domestic Series securities. Intragovernmental Holdings are primarily Government Account Series securities held by federal government trust funds, revolving funds, and special funds. As of June 30, 2012, the total federal debt outstanding was $15.9 trillion, of which $11.1 trillion was Debt Held by the Public and $4.8 trillion was Intragovernmental Holdings. The interest expense on the federal debt for fiscal year 2011 was $454 billion. Interest expense for fiscal year 2012, as of June 30, 2012, was $375.9 billion.

BFS's operations depend on modernized electronic and information system technology. Implemented by BPD in 2002, the TreasuryDirect system maintains approximately 1.3 million accounts. We have not conducted any recent performance audits of programs for managing the public debt.

Treasury, through BFS, also provides central payment services to federal agencies, operates the federal government's collections and deposit systems, provides government-wide accounting and reporting services (including preparation of the Financial Report of the United States Government), and manages collection of delinquent debt owed the federal government.

One of BFS's primary goals is to provide reliable and accurate processing of federal payments, which is an essential part of supporting the U.S. economy. These payments total over $2.4 trillion annually.

BFS issues over a billion payments a year by paper check, electronic funds transfer, and Fedwire. BFS also collects approximately $3.1 trillion a year through approximately 10,000 financial institutions. Nearly $2.9 trillion of this amount is collected electronically. Since enactment of the Debt Collection Improvement Act of 1996, Treasury, through FMS, collected about $54 billion in delinquent debt. Prompt referral of eligible delinquent debts to Treasury by federal program agencies is critical to the success of collection efforts. In fiscal year 2011, $5.5 billion of delinquent debt, including economic recovery payments, was collected.

Potential Integrity Risks

Integrity risks associated with government-wide financial services and debt management, affecting BFS include fraud and abuse by means of (1) unauthorized access to sensitive information, (2) filing false applications and claims, (3) providing false statements to obtain federal assistance or funds, (4) diversion of benefit proceeds, (5) check forgery, (6) promised services not delivered, and (7) misuse and mismanagement of federal funds. Furthermore, program risks related to this issue area include the inability to collect debt, inability to recover in a disaster, misallocation of program costs, and disruption of the federal payment function and service to the public. The changing nature of crime and recent technological innovations require that law enforcement look for and implement new ways to identify and prevent future criminal activities.

To minimize potential integrity risks, OIG plans to explore the use of data-mining methods to analyze BFS payments to reveal hidden patterns relating to trends, relationships, and correlations between the data. These data have the potential to reveal trends and patterns that could identify ongoing fraud and abuse directed against or occurring within BFS.

In-Progress and Planned Fiscal Year 2013 Projects

Controls Over the Debit Card Program for Social Security and Other Federal Benefits (In-Progress)

BFS manages a debit card program to provide unbanked federal benefit recipients the option of receiving their federal benefit payments via a debit card. The Direct Express Debit Card Program is operated by Comerica and provides an electronic funds transfer alternative for unbanked Social Security and Supplemental Security Income and other federal beneficiaries.

We plan to determine whether controls related to debit card recipient data are adequate and whether sound acquisition practices were followed to select the financial agent.

Controls Over Routing Transit Numbers (In-Progress)

FRB establishes and assigns routing transit numbers to federal agencies, including Treasury.

We plan to determine whether internal controls related to routing transit numbers assigned to BFS are effective to prevent and detect misuse of these numbers.

Administrative Resource Center User Fee Collection and Reimbursable Agreements (In-Progress)

The BFS Administrative Resource Center's mission is to provide administrative support—including accounting, travel, personnel management, and procurement services—to various federal agencies. The Administrative Resource Center operates as a franchise fund and therefore does not receive appropriated funds. Instead, it charges customers for services provided. The Administrative Resource Center has 17 Treasury customers and 59 non-Treasury customers.

We plan to determine whether the Administrative Resource Center has appropriate service agreements and a proper accounting system to (1) operate independently of BFS appropriated funding, (2) ensure proper and timely reimbursement by federal agencies for its services, and (3) account for the full costs it incurs to provide services.

BPD and FMS Consolidation (In-Progress)

We will determine whether Treasury has a comprehensive plan to accomplish the consolidation and re-designation of BPD and FMS as BFS and determine how well Treasury followed its plan. We will also determine the reliability of projected cost savings resulting from the consolidation.

Use of Permanent and Indefinite Appropriation Funds

We plan to determine whether selected permanent and indefinite appropriation funds at BFS are used in accordance with the underlying legislation.

Delinquent Debt Referrals

Prompt referral of eligible debt to BFS by federal program agencies is critical to the success of collection efforts.

We plan to evaluate BFS's efforts to ensure that creditor federal agencies refer delinquent nontax debt in accordance with the Debt Collection Improvement Act.

Department Referrals to BFS's Treasury Offset Program

We plan to determine whether the Office of Financial Stability and Office of Financial Institutions are reporting delinquent debts to the Treasury Offset Program in accordance with the Debt Collection Improvement Act of 1996, including missed TARP dividend and interest payments and any delinquent payments to SBLF.

Oversight of Lockbox Operations

BFS selects financial institutions to provide lockbox remittance services for federal agencies. Lockbox processing was adopted to accelerate deposits to Treasury's General Account at the Federal Reserve Bank of New York. Agencies instruct remitters to mail payments directly to a Treasury-designated lockbox bank. The bank processes remittance advices according to Treasury and agency instructions and transfers deposits daily to Federal Reserve Bank of New York for credit to agency accounts. Treasury compensates lockbox banks for their services. For fiscal year 2011, total lockbox collections were approximately $337 billion, of which nontax collections were $29 billion.

We plan to assess BFS's oversight of lockbox financial agents.

Survey of Debt Check Program

Debt Check is an Internet-based system intended to assist agencies with preventing delinquent debtors from obtaining new loans, loan guarantees, or loan insurance. Agencies can search the Debt Check database to determine whether assistance applicants owe delinquent nontax debt to the federal government or are delinquent with child support. Rollout of Debt Check was completed in 2004, and six agencies are using the system.

We plan to perform a survey of the Debt Check program and related controls to identify risk areas that should be audited in more depth.

Implementation of the Do Not Pay Program

Treasury initiated the Do Not Pay List program as part of the Presidential Memorandum, "Enhancing Payment Accuracy Through a Do Not Pay List," dated June 18, 2010, directing agencies to review current pre-payment and pre-award procedures and ensuring that a thorough review of available databases with relevant information on eligibility occurs before federal funds are disbursed. The Do No Pay Business Center is a Treasury program designed to give critical information to paying agencies to help reduce improper payments. To assist agencies with achieving this goal, the Do Not Pay Business Center provides two services to agencies: the Do Not Pay Portal and Do Not Pay Data Analytics Service. Each agency can choose to use any combination of these Do Not Pay services in order to best meet their needs.

The Do Not Pay portal provides users with a single entry point to search for entities that may be listed in a variety of data sources such as: the List of Excluded Individuals/Entities, Social Security Administration's Death Master File, Central Contractor Registry, Excluded Parties List System and Debt Check. Three types of searches will be available so agencies can customize use of the portal to align with their business needs: online, batch, and continuous monitoring.

We plan to assess the Do Not Pay Business Center's role in assisting federal agencies in reducing improper payments.

State Reciprocal Program Initiative

The Debt Collection Improvement Act of 1996 allows states to enter into reciprocal agreements with Treasury to collect unpaid state debt by offset of federal nontax payments, and the federal government to collect delinquent federal nontax debt by offset of state payments.

We plan to assess BFS's use of reciprocal agreements with states.

Validation of Vendor Identity

We plan to determine whether BFS ensures federal payment agencies provide correct Taxpayer Identification Numbers on payment requests as required by the Debt Collection Improvement Act of 1996.

Survey of the Federal Financing Bank

Created by Congress in 1973, the Federal Financing Bank is a government corporation under the general supervision of the Secretary of the Treasury. Its mission is to reduce the costs of federal and federally assisted borrowings, to coordinate those borrowings with federal fiscal policy, and to ensure that those borrowings are done in ways least disruptive to private markets. To accomplish this mission, the Federal Financing Bank has broad statutory authority to purchase obligations issued, sold, or guaranteed by federal agencies.

We plan to perform a survey of the Federal Financing Bank to identify areas that, based on our assessment of risk, should be audited in more depth.

Projects Under Consideration for Future Fiscal Years

Survey of Electronic Collection Methods

We plan to determine what actions BFS has taken to increase the use of electronic collections and lower the cost of collections.

Controls Over the Treasury Check Information System

The Treasury Check Information System records and reconciles the issuance and payment of Treasury checks and allows end users to query Treasury's Payments, Claims and Enhanced Reconciliation system for claim status on Automated Clearing House payments. The system enables agencies to access all claim information in one system and is accessible through a standard web browser. The Treasury Check Information System was fully implemented in June 2006.

We plan to determine whether (1) BFS implemented appropriate security controls over the Treasury Check Information System and (2) the system is achieving its intended purposes.

Survey of the Invoice Processing Platform

The Invoice Processing Platform is an Internet-based payment information portal provided by BFS for use, free of charge, to federal agencies and their vendors. It was established to improve the flow of information between federal agencies and suppliers by providing a centralized location to exchange electronic purchase orders, invoices, and related payment information. The system is available to all federal agencies and their suppliers.

We plan to gain an understanding of security measures and controls BFS uses for the portal to identify areas that, based on our assessment of risk, should be audited in more depth.

Financial Agents

We plan to assess Treasury's use of financial agency agreements to obtain services from financial institutions.

Management of Interchange Fees

In fiscal year 2011, Treasury, through FMS, collected approximately $10.2 billion in revenue through credit and debit cards and paid interchange fees of approximately $139.5 million. Interchange fees are payments that card-acquiring banks make to banks that issued the cards.

We plan to determine whether BFS is managing costs associated with interchange fees. During this audit, we plan to follow up on findings and recommendations from GAO's 2008 report, *Credit and Debit Cards: Federal Entities Are Taking Actions to Limit Their Interchange Fees, but Additional Revenue Collection Cost Savings May Exist,* (GAO-08-558; May 15, 2008).

Survey of TreasuryDirect

TreasuryDirect allows investors to conduct investment and account management activities online through a single portfolio account. TreasuryDirect has approximately 1.3 million accounts and contains personal information on customers.

We plan to assess BFS's controls over TreasuryDirect to detect and prevent fraud.

Survey of Treasury Securities Programs

BFS uses public auctions to sell marketable Treasury-issued securities to institutional and individual investors. In this regard, four types of securities are offered—bills, notes, bonds, and inflation-protected securities—and 269 public auctions were conducted in 2011. Treasury auctions occur on a set schedule and include three steps: (1) announcement of the auction, (2) bidding, and (3) issuance of the purchased securities. Our last examination of the auction process for Treasury securities was in 2000.

We plan to perform a survey of the auction process for Treasury securities and related controls to identify areas that, based on our assessment of risk, should be audited in more depth.

Controls Over the Check Forgery Insurance Fund

The Check Forgery Insurance Fund is a revolving fund administered by BFS to settle claims of non-receipt of Treasury checks. The fund's purpose is to ensure that the intended payees, whose checks were fraudulently negotiated, receive settlement in a timely manner. The OIG Office of Investigation is currently involved in a joint initiative with BFS in an effort to combat Treasury check fraud.

We plan to assess the controls over this fund.

Safety, Soundness, and Accessibility of Financial Services

Issue Area Discussion

One of Treasury's strategic objectives is to provide a flexible legal and regulatory framework that ensures a safe and sound national financial system promoting the growth of financial services, access to financial services, and fair treatment of banking customers. The most sweeping change in the regulatory framework, Dodd-Frank, enacted in July 2010, represents a significant change in the nation's financial services industry.

Dodd-Frank affects all financial regulatory agencies, including OCC, and two offices that it established within Treasury—Office of Financial Research and the Federal Insurance Office.[2] In addition, on July 21, 2011, the act required the transfer of powers, duties, and functions of the former OTS to OCC, FDIC, and FRB.

The Office of Financial Research, established by Title I of Dodd-Frank, is tasked with supporting the activities of Financial Stability Oversight Council and its member agencies by performing activities including collecting data on behalf of the council, providing such data to the council and member agencies, standardizing the types and formats of data reported and collected, and performing essential long-term research. The Federal Insurance Office, established by Title V of Dodd-Frank, is tasked with addressing problems and concerns in the regulation of insurers that could contribute to a systemic crisis in the insurance industry or the U.S. financial system.

OCC funds its operations largely through assessments levied on the financial institutions and from various licensing fees. OCC is responsible for licensing, regulating, and supervising nearly 1,400 nationally chartered banks, 640 federal savings associations, and 50 federal branches or agencies of foreign banks. OCC-supervised banks hold over $9.6 trillion in commercial banking assets and its federal savings associations hold $932 billion in total assets. OCC has over 3,700 employees located throughout the U.S.

OCC has four strategic goals: (1) a safe and sound national banking and thrift system; (2) fair access to financial services and fair treatment of customers; (3) a flexible legal and regulatory framework that enables their respective industries to provide a full competitive array of financial services; and (4) an expert, highly motivated, and diverse workforce.

From September 2007 to June 30, 2012, 447 commercial banks and federal savings associations failed, resulting in an estimated $84.6 billion in losses to the Deposit Insurance Fund. Of these 447 failures, 125 were banks or federal savings associations regulated by OCC and/or the former OTS. Our office is mandated by section 38(k) of the Federal Deposit Insurance Act to review and produce a written report on failures of OCC-regulated financial institutions that result in material losses to the

---

[2] Dodd-Frank also established two other offices within Treasury—the Offices of Minority and Women Inclusion in Departmental Offices and OCC.

fund. The law also requires that the report be completed within 6 months after it becomes apparent that a material loss has incurred. Dodd-Frank established the threshold loss amount triggering a material loss review to $150 million for 2012 and 2013, and $50 million in 2014 and thereafter, with a provision for increasing the threshold to $75 million under certain circumstances. To date, during the recent economic downturn, we have completed 54 material loss reviews.

Dodd-Frank also requires that for any failure of a OCC-regulated bank or thrift with a loss to the Deposit Insurance Fund under the threshold triggering a mandated material loss review, that we conduct a review that is limited to determining (1) the grounds identified by OCC for appointing FDIC as receiver, and (2) whether any unusual circumstances exist that might warrant an in-depth review of the loss.

In-Progress and Planned Fiscal Year 2013 Projects

Reviews of Failed OCC-Regulated Financial Institutions (In-Progress)

The purpose of a material loss review is to provide (1) an independent analysis of why the institution failed and resulted in a material loss; (2) evaluate the relevant regulator's supervision of the institution; and (3) as appropriate, make recommendations to prevent similar losses in the future. The reviews are performed by OIG staff. As of the date of this plan, no material loss reviews were in progress.

For failed financial institutions with estimated losses under the material loss review threshold, we will (1) determine the grounds identified by OCC for appointing FDIC as receiver; and (2) determine whether any unusual circumstances exist that might warrant an in-depth review of the loss. To date, during the recent economic downturn, we have completed 59 limited reviews and are engaged in 4 others.

Transfer of OTS Functions (Ongoing)

Title III, Section 327 of Dodd-Frank requires that Treasury OIG, FDIC OIG, and FRB OIG jointly review the transfer of the functions, employees, funds, and property of OTS to FRB, FDIC, and OCC. In accordance with Title III, the transfer occurred in July 2011. Our first joint review, completed in March 2011, determined that the Joint Implementation Plan (Plan) for the transfer prepared by FRB, FDIC, OCC, and OTS conformed to relevant Title III provisions with one exception, which was corrected by an amendment to the Plan. After the initial joint review of the Plan, Section 327 requires that every 6 months we jointly provide a written report on the status of the implementation of the Plan. As of September 2012, we issued three reports under this requirement. In these reports, we concluded that FRB, FDIC, OCC, and OTS implemented the actions in the Plan that were necessary to transfer OTS functions, employees, and funds to FRB, FDIC, and OCC, and procedures and safeguards are in place as outlined in the Plan to ensure transferred employees are not unfairly disadvantaged. However, there are certain other items related to the Plan that are ongoing or are not yet required to be completed as provided in Title III.

In accordance with Section 327, we and the OIGs of FRB and FDIC will monitor and jointly report every 6 months on the implementation of the Plan until all aspects have been implemented.

Supervision of Bank Processes to Prevent, Detect, and Report Criminal Activity by Bank Employees (In-Progress)

We plan to (1) identify the extent and nature of criminal and other suspicious activity committed by bank and thrift employees reported to FinCEN under the BSA through a review of Suspicious Activity Reports and related analytical studies; (2) identify OCC examination procedures to ensure national banks and federal savings associations have sufficient processes to prevent, detect, and report internal criminal activities; (3) determine whether the procedures are applied effectively; and (4) determine whether deficiencies identified during the examination process result in appropriate supervisory actions which are tracked and satisfactorily resolved.

Protection of Financial Services Sector Critical Infrastructure (In-Progress)

We plan to determine the effectiveness of Treasury's coordination efforts with private sector entities and other government entities to protect the banking and finance portions of the nation's critical infrastructure.

Lessons Learned from Bank Failures (In-Progress)

We plan to review completed material loss reviews and other reviews of Treasury-regulated failed financial institutions to (1) identify common themes related to the causes of failure and supervision of institutions, and (2) assess OCC's actions to strengthen the supervisory process in response to our audit recommendations as well as other initiatives by OCC.

Oversight of Foreclosure-Related Consent Orders (In-Progress)

In April 2011, OCC issued formal enforcement actions against eight national bank mortgage servicers and two third-party service providers for unsafe and unsound practices related to residential mortgage loan servicing and foreclosure processing. The eight servicers were Bank of America, Citibank, HSBC, JPMorgan Chase, MetLife Bank, PNC, U.S. Bank, and Wells Fargo. The two service providers are Lender Processing Services and MERSCORP. The enforcement actions require the servicers to promptly correct deficiencies in residential mortgage loan servicing and foreclosure practices that examiners identified in reviews conducted during the fourth quarter of 2010.

The actions require the servicers to make significant improvements in practices for residential mortgage loan servicing and foreclosure processing, including communications with borrowers and dual-tracking, which occurs when servicers continue to pursue foreclosure during the loan modification process. The enforcement actions require the servicers to ensure that foreclosures are not pursued once a mortgage has been approved for modification and to establish a single point of contact for borrowers throughout the loan modification and foreclosure processes. In addition, the actions require servicers to establish robust oversight and controls pertaining to their third-party vendors, including outside legal counsel, that provide default management or foreclosure services. OCC's actions also require each servicer to engage an independent firm to conduct a multi-faceted review of foreclosure actions between January 1, 2009, and December 31, 2010. This requirement includes a comprehensive "look back" to assess whether foreclosures complied with federal and state laws, whether foreclosures occurred when grounds for foreclosure were not present, such as when loans were performing, and whether any errors, misrepresentations or other deficiencies resulted in financial injury to borrowers. The actions also require each servicer to establish a process for borrowers who believe they have been financially harmed by such deficiencies to make submissions to be considered for remediation. Each servicer must also submit a plan to remediate all financial injury to borrowers caused by any errors, misrepresentations, or other deficiencies identified in the independent consultant's findings.

We plan to assess (1) OCC's oversight of servicers' efforts to comply with foreclosure related consent orders; (2) OCC's determination of qualifications and independence of consultants hired by servicers in accordance with the consent orders; (3) OCC's oversight of consultants' efforts to perform outreach, conduct file reviews, and review homeowner claims of financial harm; and (4) OCC's oversight of the single integrated claims process established by OCC, servicers, and the consultants.

Review of the Establishment and Effectiveness of the Federal Insurance Office (In-Progress)

We plan to determine the status and effectiveness of Treasury's process to establish the Federal Insurance Office.

Supervision of Bank Trading Activities (In-Progress)

We plan to determine and assess OCC's process to supervise bank trading activities. We plan to initially focus on OCC's supervision of J.P. Morgan Chase, National Association.

Examination Coverage of Third-Party Service Providers (In-Progress)

We plan to assess OCC's examinations of third-party service providers used by OCC regulated banks.

Separation of Funds and Activities

Consistent with a directive in House Report 112-550, we plan as assess the separation of funds and activities between mandatory-funded offices, such as the Office of Financial Research and the Office of Financial Stability, and discretionary-funded offices that carry out related or overlapping work, such as Treasury's Office of Domestic Finance or Office of Economic Policy. We also plan during this review to assess the Office of Financial Research's procurement activities.

Examination Coverage of Identity Theft Risk at Financial Institutions

We plan to determine whether OCC examinations of financial institutions are adequate to address privacy risks, including identity theft.

Supervision of Consumer Financial Protection and Compliance

We plan to assess OCC's (1) supervision over consumer protection and compliance at OCC-regulated financial institutions; and (2) coordination with the Consumer Financial Protection Bureau and processing of consumer complaints involving national banks and federal savings associations with more than $10 billion in assets to facilitate the transition of the responsibilities of these complaints to the bureau.

Supervision of Financial Institutions' Other Real Estate Owned Property

We plan to evaluate OCC's supervision of other real estate owned property in financial institutions. Our specific objectives are to determine whether (1) guidance promoting effective assessment and control of other real estate owned property has been promulgated; (2) existing OCC monitoring, risk assessment, and examination procedures are sufficient to address other real estate owned property risk; (3) the procedures are applied effectively; and (4) deficiencies identified by OCC result in appropriate supervisory actions which are tracked and satisfactorily resolved.

OCC's Licensing and Charter Approval Process

We plan to (1) determine the licensing and charter conversion process for financial institutions, (2) determine the criteria used by OCC to make licensing and charter conversion decisions, and (3) verify OCC's compliance with guidelines when making approval decisions.

Supervision of Student Loan Products

We plan to assess OCC's supervision to ensure financial institutions conduct student loan lending activities in a safe and sound manner.

Supervision of Foreign Country Risk

We plan to evaluate OCC's supervision of financial institutions' international exposures. Our specific objectives are to determine whether (1) guidance promoting effective assessment and control of national banks' country risk has been promulgated; (2) existing OCC monitoring, risk assessment and examination procedures are sufficient to address country risk; (3) the procedures have been applied effectively; and (4) deficiencies identified during the examination process result in appropriate supervisory actions which are tracked and satisfactorily resolved.

Supervision of Federal Branches of Foreign Banks

We plan to assess OCC's supervision of foreign banking organizations operating in the U.S.

Supervision of Interest Rate Risk

We plan to assess OCC's examination coverage related to financial institutions' risk management over interest rate risk.

Legal Entity Identifier Implementation

We plan to assess progress made by the Office of Financial Research to implement the Legal Entity Identifier as the universal standard for identifying all parties to financial contracts.

Office of Financial Research Performance Measures

We plan to assess the design and implementation of performance measures by the Office of Financial Research.

Supervision of Incentive-Based Compensation Provisions of Dodd-Frank

Section 956 of Dodd-Frank requires financial institutions, with total consolidated assets of $1 billion or more, to disclose to the appropriate regulator the structures of all incentive-based compensation arrangements. The disclosure should allow the regulator to determine whether the incentive-based compensation structure (1) provides executives, employees, directors, or principal shareholders with excessive compensation, fees or benefits or (2) could lead to material financial losses to the financial institution. Further, the law requires the federal regulators to jointly prescribe regulations or guidelines to provide for the disclosure of compensation arrangements and to prohibit any types of incentive-based payment arrangement that encourages inappropriate risks by the covered financial institution.

Once the final rules are in place, we plan to assess, OCC's supervision of incentive-based compensation structures in OCC-regulated financial institutions and determine whether: (1) OCC monitoring, risk assessment and examination procedures are sufficient to ensure bank's compliance with these requirements; (2) the procedures are applied effectively; and (3) deficiencies identified by OCC result in appropriate supervisory actions which are tracked and satisfactorily resolved.

Development, Training, Rotation, and Performance Evaluations of OCC Examiners

We plan to assess OCC processes for developing, training, rotating, and evaluating the performance of bank examiners.

Projects Under Consideration for Future Fiscal Years

Supervision of Small Banks

We plan to assess the safety and soundness challenges facing small banks and OCC's supervisory response to those challenges. Preliminarily, our focus will be on institutions with total assets of $250 million or less.

OCC Enforcement Practices

We plan to assess OCC's enforcement practices, including (1) the factors used to determine the use of formal and informal enforcement actions; (2) the timeliness of enforcement actions; (3) controls to ensure consistency in the use of enforcement actions; and (4) the manner in which OCC ensures compliance with enforcement actions.

Supervisory Use of Individual Minimum Capital Requirements

We plan to assess how OCC applies capital restrictions and risk-weighting to institutions they supervise to include (1) OCC's use of individual minimum capital requirements as an enforcement action, (2) the criteria used to calculate the capital requirement, and (3) how the minimum capital requirements are enforced.

Office of Financial Research Assessment Process

We plan to determine whether the Office of Financial Research's (1) assessment methodology is being implemented in accordance with Section 155 of Dodd-Frank and the related regulation and (2) assessments are collected and used to fund the office's mission and provide support to the Financial Stability Oversight Council.

Implementation of Interagency Appraisal and Evaluation Guidelines

We plan to assess OCC's oversight of the implementation of the Interagency Appraisal and Evaluation Guidelines of Section 1472 of Dodd-Frank.

OCC's Participation in the Shared National Credit Program

We plan to evaluate OCC's participation in the Shared National Credit Program. Our specific objectives are to (1) identify the guidance promoting effective review of shared national credits; (2) determine whether existing monitoring, risk assessment and examination procedures are sufficient to address risk to the banking industry by shared national credits; (3) determine whether the procedures are applied effectively; and (4) determine whether deficiencies identified during the examination process resulted in appropriate supervisory actions which are tracked and satisfactorily resolved.

Supervision of Large Institutions

We plan to assess OCC examinations of institutions with assets exceeding $100 billion.

Safeguards Over Financial Institutions' Sensitive Information

We plan to determine whether OCC examiners adhere to applicable laws, regulations, and policies and procedures for safeguarding the privacy and confidentiality of sensitive information financial institutions provide to OCC during the examination process.

Supervision of Nonbanking Activities of Financial Institutions

We plan to assess OCC supervision of nonbanking activities of regulated financial institutions and their affiliates.

OCC's Alternatives to the Use of Credit Ratings

Section 939A of Dodd-Frank contains two directives to federal agencies including the OCC. First, section 939A directs all federal agencies to review, no later than 1 year after enactment, any regulation that requires the use of an assessment of creditworthiness of a security or money market instrument and any references to, or requirements in, such regulations regarding credit ratings. Second, the agencies are required to remove any references to, or requirements of reliance on, credit ratings and substitute such standard of creditworthiness as each agency determines is appropriate. The statute further provides that the agencies shall seek to establish, to the extent feasible, uniform standards of creditworthiness, taking into account the entities the agencies regulate and the purposes for which those entities would rely on such standards.

We plan to assess OCC's implementation of guidance on alternatives to the use of credit ratings by financial institutions to determine the creditworthiness of securities and money market instruments.

Federal Insurance Office Performance Measures

We plan to assess the design and implementation of performance measures by the Federal Insurance Office.

Commercial Real Estate Concentrations

We plan to determine the risks associated with financial institutions having high commercial real estate concentrations and related OCC supervisory approaches.

Revenue Collection and Industry Regulation

Issue Area Discussion

TTB administers collection of federal excise taxes on tobacco products, alcohol, and firearms and ammunition. The bureau is also responsible for ensuring compliance with tobacco and alcohol permitting requirements as well as ensuring alcohol products are properly labeled, advertised, and marketed. In addition, the bureau ensures fair trade practices and facilitates the international trade of alcohol beverage products. TTB administers and enforces the (1) Internal Revenue Code pertaining to the excise taxation and authorized operations of alcohol and tobacco producers and related industries; (2) Federal Alcohol Administration Act; (3) Alcohol Beverage Labeling Act; and (4) Webb-Kenyon Act, which prohibits the shipment of alcohol beverages into a state in violation of the state's laws. The bureau is headquartered in Washington, D.C., and maintains its tax and permit processing center, the National Revenue Center, in Cincinnati, Ohio. TTB's Tax Audit Division has 6 district field office locations and its Trade Investigations Division has 6 district field offices. TTB also has alcohol and tobacco laboratories in Maryland and California.

During fiscal year 2011, TTB collected $23.5 billion in excise taxes and other revenue from about 7,750 excise taxpayers. More than 7,200 TTB taxpayers were registered to file and pay excise taxes electronically, an increase of 12 percent over the prior year. To better protect the federal revenue, TTB believes a vigorous tax enforcement program is needed. TTB used a $3 million allocation from Congress to procure special agent services from IRS to enforce TTB's criminal jurisdiction. In 8 months of active investigations in 2011, TTB opened 21 criminal cases that identified $20 million in tax liabilities. TTB estimated the return on investment was 10 to 1. TTB continued this arrangement in fiscal year 2012 with renewed funding.

TTB regulates the alcohol and tobacco industries to ensure all federal excise taxes due are collected. TTB also assures compliance with federal tobacco permitting and alcohol permitting, labeling, and marketing requirements to protect consumers. The bureau processes applications to enter into the alcohol and tobacco industries and ensures that alcohol beverages are produced, labeled, advertised, and marketed, in accordance with federal law. In fiscal year 2011, TTB launched two e-Gov systems—Permits Online and Formulas Online—to allow customers to access TTB through the Web. Permits Online was initiated to deal with staffing losses and the rising workload. TTB believes these programs have been successful. In fiscal year 2011, TTB processed approximately 26,000 new and amended permits.

The bureau also reviews labels and formulas for domestic and imported beverage alcohol products and maintains public access to approved Certificates of Label Approval, which are required for every alcoholic beverage. In fiscal year 2011, the bureau received and processed over 145,000 applications. TTB monitors labeling compliance through the Alcohol Beverage Sampling Program and tests samples of wine, distilled spirits, and malt beverages for content in its in-house laboratories.

In addition to its tax and regulatory functions, TTB helps facilitate global alcohol trade, including exports of wine and spirits that most recently totaled approximately $2.2 billion. In fiscal year 2011, TTB entered into international agreements with Italy, France, and Canada, among others. To ensure that the commercial trade of alcohol beverages is fair and open to all, TTB reached a $1.9 million settlement in a series of cases in which TTB alleged that six major alcohol beverage suppliers were furnishing illegal inducements to a retail casino chain in return for preferential shelf space for their products. This was the largest set of offers of compromise ever accepted by TTB for trade practice violations.

The Secretary of the Treasury has authority for Customs revenue functions, and this oversight is carried out by the Office of Tax Policy. The Homeland Security Act of 2002 transferred the former U.S. Customs Service from Treasury to the Department of Homeland Security in March 2003, where it became Customs and Border Protection. However, as provided by the act, Treasury retained sole authority to approve any regulations concerning import quotas or trade bans, user fees, marking, labeling, copyright and trademark enforcement, and the completion of entry or substance of entry summary, including duty assignment and collection, classification, valuation, application of the U.S. Harmonized Tariff Schedules, eligibility or requirements for preferential trade programs, and the establishment of related recordkeeping requirements. Treasury also reviews Customs and Border Protection rulings involving these topics if they constitute a change in practice.

Because our resources were devoted to mandated work related principally to failed banks for the last several years, we have not been able to devote the attention to this area that we believe necessary. In fiscal year 2012, we initiated our first performance audit at TTB since 2006. Resources permitting, we plan to increase our audit activity in TTB in fiscal year 2013.

Potential Integrity Risks

The major integrity risks for TTB involve not collecting all revenue rightfully do and having alcohol products in the marketplace that are improperly labeled. The failure by industry members to pay all taxes due, either intentionally or otherwise, coupled with the risk that the TTB tax verification and audit program would not detect these underpayments, or that industry members could attempt to corrupt government officials through bribery or other means, could seriously undermine TTB's tax collection activity. Similarly, fraudulent manufacturers or distributors could attempt to place untaxed, unsafe, or deceptively advertised products into the marketplace.

Notwithstanding the attractiveness of evading alcohol taxes through product diversion and smuggling, the passage of the Children's Health Insurance Program Reauthorization Act of 2009 (CHIPRA) provided added incentive to evade tobacco taxes. Specifically, CHIPRA increased the federal excise tax on all tobacco products, including an increase of more than 150 percent on cigarettes. CHIPRA required Treasury to conduct a study concerning the magnitude of illicit tobacco trade in the U.S. The study found that accurately measuring the amount of federal tax receipts lost as a result of tobacco diversion and smuggling was difficult (due to its inherently clandestine nature), but that significant losses could be occurring. TTB's 2011 annual report estimated federal excise tax losses due to illicit cigarette trade could range from $500 million to $1.5 billion and that the losses would be significantly higher using the post-CHIPRA tax rates. The study also identified several weaknesses in the control of tobacco products which can directly affect tax collection. While manufacturers and importers of tobacco products and processed tobacco must have permits to operate and are subject to recordkeeping requirements, the same is not true of tobacco brokers, wholesalers and retailers of tobacco products. Also, access to machinery used to manufacture cigarettes is unrestricted and may be used to violate the tax code.

Although the Prevent All Cigarette Trafficking Act of 2010 addressed some of these risks, Internet sales remain an area of concern for TTB's revenue collection responsibilities, as the bureau must coordinate with the U.S. Postal Service and ground carriers for enforcement assistance.

In-Progress and Planned Fiscal Year 2013 Projects

Tax Receipts Lost Due to Illicit Trade (In-Progress)

Section 703 of CHIPRA directed the Secretary of the Treasury to conduct a study concerning the magnitude of illicit tobacco trade in the U.S. and to submit to Congress a report with recommendations for the most effective steps to reduce illicit tobacco trade. The resulting Treasury study used a "tax gap" analysis to determine the magnitude of tax receipts lost and included three recommendations to address this issue.

We plan to assess actions taken by TTB in response to the Treasury study or other actions taken to mitigate tax losses. We also plan to determine if a similar tax gap analysis should be used to identify tax receipts lost due to illicit alcohol trade.

TTB Controls Over the Alcohol and Tobacco Permit Program

We plan to determine whether TTB has effective controls to ensure that alcohol and tobacco permits are issued only to qualified persons and businesses and assess TTB's efforts to identify and obtain permits from tobacco processors over which the bureau now has regulatory authority. As part of this work, we plan to assess TTB's "Permits Online" program.

Effect of CHIPRA on Tax Paid Removals of Tobacco Products

Federal excise taxes are imposed on tobacco products when they are removed for sale from manufacturers or when they are imported into the U.S. In 2009, CHIPRA significantly increased the tax rates on all tobacco products. The tax rates for pipe tobacco and roll-your-own tobacco, previously taxed at similar rates, were increased to $2.83 per pound and $24.78 per pound, respectively. TTB's analysis of the tobacco industry identified a dramatic shift in the reported removals of roll-your-own tobacco in favor of lower taxed pipe tobacco. TTB also identified an immediate shift in the cigar market from small cigars to lower taxed large cigars. Revenue loss estimates associated with these transitions may exceed $1 billion.

We plan to assess TTB's efforts to ensure all appropriate taxes are paid, and determine the impact of CHIPRA tax increases on reported removals of other products such as large and small cigars that are subject to different tax rates.

Projects Under Consideration for Future Fiscal Years

TTB's Tax Verification Process

TTB's tax verification process incorporates a strategic risk-based approach to conduct targeted compliance audits and investigations of industry members. In fiscal year 2011, these efforts resulted in the identification of $35 million in additional tax, penalties, and interest, and the collection of more than $15 million.

We plan to evaluate TTB's excise tax verification process.

TTB Designation of American Viticultural Areas

An American Viticultural Area is a designated wine-grape-growing region with features that affect the growing conditions of the area (climate, soil, elevation, physical features) and that distinguish it from surrounding areas.

We plan to assess the controls in place over TTB's program to designate American Viticultural Areas.

TTB's Use of Collection Procedures and Offers in Compromise to Collect Revenue

TTB uses offers in compromise to collect outstanding taxes due in lieu of civil or criminal proceedings.

We plan to determine whether TTB has effective collection procedures for delinquent accounts. We also plan to assess TTB's use of offers in compromise in its collection activities.

TTB Alcohol and Tobacco Laboratory Services

We plan to determine whether TTB alcohol and tobacco laboratories are providing timely and responsive service to TTB program units. As part of the audit, we plan to evaluate TTB's efforts to ensure the safety of imported beverage products through pre-import activities, post-market sampling, and laboratory analysis.

Coordinating Participation in the International Trade Data System Project

The SAFE Port Act formally established the International Trade Data System, a system for processing imports and exports. The system is operated by Customs and Border Protection in collaboration with 43 agencies. The act gave the Secretary of the Treasury responsibility for coordinating interagency participation in the system. One of its features allows TTB to review data on importations of alcohol and tobacco through the Customs and Border Protection automated commercial environment portal. TTB is also to provide Customs and Border Protection access to its database of approved alcohol labels, which will allow Customs inspectors to compare the approved labels with the actual labels on the imported products.

We plan to determine whether Treasury is fulfilling its responsibility under the SAFE Port Act. We also plan to determine whether the information sharing between TTB and Customs has proved beneficial in ensuring only approved products are imported.

TTB Controls Over Cover-Over Payments

Taxes collected on rum produced in Puerto Rico or the U.S. Virgin Islands and transported to the U.S. are covered over to the territory where the rum is produced. Taxes collected on rum imported into the U.S. from foreign countries are also covered over to the two territories; the payments are split between Puerto Rico and the U.S. Virgin Islands. In fiscal year 2011, TTB processed $462 million of these cover-over reimbursements to the treasuries of Puerto Rico and the U.S. Virgin Islands combined, representing increases of 20 and 8 percent, respectively, over fiscal year 2010 cover-over reimbursements.

We plan to determine whether TTB's controls ensure that cover-over reimbursements are made for the correct amounts and in a timely manner.

TTB's Efforts to Ensure the Accurate Collection of Federal Excise Taxes on Imports

We plan to assess TTB's efforts to identify federal excise taxes due on undeclared and misclassified alcohol and tobacco product imports and TTB's coordination with the Customs and Border Patrol to ensure all federal excise taxes due are paid by importers.

TTB Reviews of Manufacturer Nonbeverage Drawback Claims

When a manufacturer uses alcohol to produce a food, flavor, medicine, or perfume that is approved by TTB's Nonbeverage Products Laboratory as unfit for beverage purposes, the manufacturer can claim a return, or drawback, on most of the distilled spirits excise tax paid. In fiscal year 2011, approved nonbeverage drawback claims totaled $307 million.

We plan to assess TTB's review of nonbeverage product manufacturer claims.

TTB Use of Collateral to Protect Revenue

TTB protects excise tax revenue by mandating that taxpayers pledge collateral—such as a bond, note, or securities—to offset tax liability if payments are not made.

We plan to determine whether TTB is ensuring that taxpayers maintain adequate collateral to protect tax revenue.

TTB Online Certificate of Label Approval

We plan to determine whether TTB's online label approval system is operating as intended.

TTB's Regulatory Oversight of Manufacturers of Processed Tobacco

CHIPRA established TTB's responsibility for oversight of manufacturers of processed tobacco. These manufacturers receive tobacco plants from growers, remove the stems, and cut the tobacco leaves. The processed tobacco is used by manufacturers that produce tobacco products such as cigarettes and cigars. Both domestically grown and imported processed tobacco is generally not subject to federal excise tax until manufactured into tobacco products and removed for consumption in the U.S. In 2010, the market for processed tobacco was approximately 1.1 billion pounds. Manufacturers of processed tobacco can legally sell processed tobacco to product manufacturers, other businesses that further process the tobacco, or tobacco brokers, many of whom are not licensed to operate by TTB. Manufacturers of processed tobacco are required to report to TTB sales of processed tobacco to businesses without TTB permits. Because of regulatory restrictions, TTB cannot always follow the processed tobacco through the industry pipeline to determine what products the processed tobacco was manufactured into and if federal excise taxes were paid.

We plan to (1) determine what actions TTB has taken to regulate manufacturers of processed tobacco, (2) determine how TTB has used its authority to detect and prevent processed tobacco from entering the illicit market, and (3) identify regulatory restrictions limiting TTB's ability to prevent illicit tobacco trade related to processed tobacco.

Bill and Coin Manufacturing, Marketing, and Distribution Operations

Issue Area Discussion

BEP produces U.S. currency and other security documents issued by the federal government. BEP also processes claims for the redemption of mutilated paper currency and provides technical assistance and advice to other federal agencies on the design and production of documents requiring counterfeit deterrence. BEP has production facilities in Washington, D.C., and Fort Worth, Texas.

In fiscal year 2011, BEP delivered 5.8 billion Federal Reserve notes to the FRBs compared to the 6.4 billion delivered in fiscal year 2010. BEP planned to deliver the redesigned NexGen $100 notes to FRB in late 2010 for the anticipated public release in February 2011. However, problems in the production process of these notes delayed the release date. BEP is currently working with stakeholders and hopes to resume full production on the NexGen $100 note in 2012.

The Mint's principal mission is to produce the nation's circulation coinage for trade and commerce. The Mint also produces commemorative and investment products for collectors and investors. In addition to its headquarters in Washington, D.C., the Mint has four production facilities located in Philadelphia, West Point, Denver, and San Francisco. It also maintains the U.S. bullion depository at Fort Knox.

In fiscal year 2011, the Mint manufactured 7.4 billion coins for the FRBs which is an increase of 37 percent compared to the 5.4 billion produced in fiscal year 2010. The Mint expects circulating coin production volumes in 2013 to increase to 8.4 billion, about a 9 percent increase over fiscal year 2012 projections. In December 2011, Treasury reported plans to suspend the circulating dollar coin production starting in fiscal year 2012 as part of the Campaign to Cut Waste and in recognition of the large holdings of dollar coins at the FRBs.

In fiscal year 1996, the Mint Public Enterprise Fund was created to enable the Mint to operate as a revolving fund. All receipts deposited into the fund are available for Mint operations and the cost of safeguarding government assets in the Mint's custody, without fiscal year limitations. Even though the Mint is not dependent on appropriated funds, its spending authority is approved by Congress each fiscal year. The Secretary of the Treasury must annually determine the amount of excess in the fund that is not needed for Mint operations for transfer to the Treasury General Fund. For fiscal year 2011, the Mint transferred $51 million to the Treasury General Fund. This amount is down significantly from years past—transferred amounts were $388 million in fiscal year 2010 and $475 million in fiscal year 2009. The Mint reported in its fiscal year 2011 annual report that it is holding cash in reserve for future potential impacts to its circulating program from the continued penny and nickel losses, and a decline in demand for the $1 coins.

Potential Weaknesses

Because their operations are financed through revolving funds, BEP and the Mint are subject to fewer congressional controls than appropriated agencies. The Mint also has greater flexibility in conducting its procurement activities. For example, the Mint is exempt from the Federal Acquisition Regulation. Continued prudent use of its fund authority flexibilities is necessary to ensure a maximum return to the Treasury General Fund.

Continuing Issue With BEP Concerning Currency Products that Cannot Be Readily Recognized by Blind and Visually Impaired Individuals

In 2006, a federal judge ruled that the Department's failure to design, produce, and issue paper currency that is readily distinguishable to blind and visually impaired individuals violated federal law. Two years later, a federal appeals court ruled that the U.S. discriminates against blind and visually impaired individuals by producing currency that they cannot recognize without the assistance of others. In conjunction with this decision and in consultation with BEP and Department of Justice attorneys, a federal judge ruled that the next generation of $5, $10, $20, and $50 notes must be manufactured so that blind and visually impaired individuals can tell them apart. This ruling did not affect the design of the new $100 note, but future designs must ensure that all denominations, except for the $1 note, be distinguishable from other notes.

Potential Integrity Risks

Past audits have noted various weaknesses in BEP's physical security. As noted in the most recent report, *Bill and Coin Manufacturing: Improved Security Over the NexGen $100 Notes is Necessary,* (OIG-11-068; May 13, 2011), management took corrective action on a serious weakness found by our auditors in the security over NexGen $100 finished notes and work-in-process sheets at both BEP's Eastern Currency Facility and Western Currency Facility. Previously in fiscal year 2008, as discussed in *Bill and Coin Manufacturing: BEP Needs to Enforce and Strengthen Controls at Its Eastern Currency Facility to Prevent and Detect Employee Theft,* (OIG-08-036; June 12, 2008), following a theft at the Eastern Currency Facility we found that BEP did not ensure that production supervisors enforced, and employees adhered to, existing internal controls. Additionally, no policies and procedures were in place to investigate production discrepancies. Issues with BEP's information security were also noted in a recent report, *BEP's Network and Systems Security Was Found to Be Insufficient,* (OIG-11-112; Sep. 30, 2011). We found BEP did not establish sufficient protection for its network and systems to protect against insider threats and noted critical vulnerabilities caused by a number of missing security patches.

In-Progress and Planned Fiscal Year 2013 Projects

BEP's Project Management of the Enterprise Network System (In-Progress)

BEP's Enterprise Network System (BEN) project is intended to simplify and standardize procedures, increase efficiency, and eliminate unnecessary processes at BEP to increase product quality, reduce spoilage, and improve accountability.

We plan to determine whether (1) the BEN project business case is based on appropriate and supportable assumptions and cost/benefit estimates, (2) sound project management principles are followed in carrying out BEN, and (3) federal regulations and guidance, Treasury directives, and BEP policies and procedures are followed in conjunction with the project.

Physical Security at Mint Facilities (In-Progress)

We plan to (1) assess the Mint's physical security policies and procedures, and (2) determine whether the facilities' physical security conforms to those policies and procedures.

Mint Controls Over the Sales of Limited-Production, Investment-Grade Products (In-Progress)

In addition to manufacturing circulating coins and numismatic products made available to the public, the Mint also sells precious metal (gold, silver and platinum) investment grade bullion coins to pre-qualified authorized purchasers for resale to the public.

We plan to determine whether the Mint has adequate controls to ensure the broadest and most fair access to its products.

Burson-Marsteller Incurred Cost Audit (In-Progress)

We plan to determine whether contractor invoicing for services and deliverables followed the terms of its public education campaign contract with BEP and the Federal Acquisition Regulation.

BEP Efforts to Produce Products for the Blind and Visually Impaired

In Senate Report 112-177 to the fiscal year 2013 Treasury appropriation bill, the Appropriations Committee directed BEP to report to Congress and to OIG within 90 days of enactment on a detailed plan, including a timeline, to develop, design, test, and print currency with accessibility features. The plan is to also include an analysis of the feasibility of expediting the federal acquisition process for the specialized equipment required to create accessibility features. The Committee further directed our office to provide an initial assessment of the plan to the Committee within 60 days of receipt and to report on its progress and implementation every 6 months thereafter until the plan is fully implemented.

In light of this pending directive, we plan to assess BEP's efforts to provide meaningful access to U.S. currency for blind and visually impaired individuals.

Mint Penny and Nickel Costs

The Mint's costs (e.g., cost of the metal, fabrication, direct and indirect expenses) to produce pennies and nickels was more than double the face value of the coins produced in fiscal year 2011. This is the fifth straight year where production costs for these coins exceeded their face values.

We plan to assess the Mint's efforts to control costs in the production of pennies and nickels.

Mint Commemorative Coin Programs

Congress authorizes commemorative coins that celebrate and honor American people, places, events, and institutions. Although these coins are legal tender, they are not intended for general circulation. The Mint produces limited quantities of commemorative coins and makes them available for a short period of time.

We plan to assess the Mint's management of the commemorative coin programs and related surcharges.

BEP's Facilities Studies and Continuity of Operations Planning

In early 2012, BEP completed a study of the infrastructure and repairs needs of the Eastern Currency Facility, which was built in the early 1900's. Within the next several years, BEP plans to coordinate with FRB to make a key decision on whether to upgrade and/or procure new facilities.

We plan to determine whether BEP's facilities study and resulting investment decisions are based on appropriate and supportable assumptions and cost/benefit estimates. We also plan to determine whether BEP comprehensively developed and tested continuity of operations plans for currency production should a major disruption occur at one or both its production facilities.

Impact of Electronic Payments to BEP and Mint

We plan to assess efforts by BEP and Mint to determine and respond to changing consumer demands for their currency and coin products.

Projects Under Consideration for Future Fiscal Years

America the Beautiful Silver Coin Program

Public Law 110-456 enacted the America the Beautiful Quarters program which also allows the Mint to manufacture silver bullion quarters coins with the same design as the circulating coins. The act requires that the bullion coins be available for sale no sooner than the first day of the calendar year in which the corresponding circulating quarter coin is issued and only during the year in which the circulating quarter coin is issued.

We plan to determine whether the Mint is effectively managing the America the Beautiful bullion coin program and ensuring compliance with Public Law 110-456, as it relates to the sales period for each coin.

Mint Order Fulfillment

We plan to determine whether the Mint implemented adequate controls for its customer service and order fulfillment process to ensure adequate customer service is provided and costs are controlled.

Mint Sales General and Administrative Expense Allocation

In 2011, the Mint reported a change to its sales, general, and administrative expenses allocation methodology intended to more accurately represent costs incurred for each coin denomination.

We plan to determine whether the Mint's recent changes to the allocation of selling, general, and administrative expenses are consistent with managerial cost accounting principles.

BEP's Capital Investment Program

We plan to determine whether BEP's capital investment program ensures that all capital needs are being identified and that sufficient funds are being allocated to meet current and future capital needs.

BEP Employee Safety

We plan to assess BEP's efforts to ensure safe working conditions in its production facilities. Separate audits are planned of the Eastern Currency Facility and Western Currency Facility.

Domestic and International Assistance Programs

Issue Area Discussion

Treasury plays an important role in a number of domestic and international assistance programs that have a significant impact on the economy. Domestic programs range from those that enhance the availability of financial education, credit, investment capital, and financial services to communities around the U.S., to programs that assist in coping with the effects of the current economic conditions. Treasury's role in these areas expanded under HERA, the Emergency Economic Stabilization Act of 2008 (which created the TARP), the Recovery Act, Dodd-Frank, and the Small Business Jobs Act of 2010.

International programs address the role of international financial institutions and promote economic stability and growth in other countries.

HERA

The purpose of the act is to address problems and concerns in the mortgage and banking industries. Among other things, the act established the Federal Housing Finance Agency (HFA) as an independent agency to oversee Fannie Mae, Freddie Mac, and the Federal Home Loan Banks (also referred to as government-sponsored enterprises). The act also established the Federal Housing Finance Oversight Board to advise the agency with respect to overall strategies and policies in carrying out its responsibilities. The Secretary of the Treasury is a member of this board. It also assigned Treasury new authorities and responsibilities. Although certain Treasury purchase authorities under HERA expired in December 2009, Treasury maintains a sizeable investment in Fannie Mae and Freddie Mac and continues to provide financial support through the Senior Preferred Purchase Agreements and the HFA Initiative.

- **Government Sponsored Enterprises** In connection with the increased federal regulatory oversight of Fannie Mae, Freddie Mac, and the Federal Home Loan Banks, the act increased Treasury's authority over existing lines of credit to the entities that gave the Secretary of the Treasury standby, unlimited authority to buy stock or debt in them. To do so, the Secretary made an emergency determination required by HERA that use of the authority was necessary to stabilize markets, prevent disruptions in mortgage availability, and protect the taxpayer. Through Senior Preferred Stock Purchase Agreements, Treasury provides financial support to Fannie Mae and Freddie Mac after any quarter that the entities report net worth deficiencies. In exchange, the liquidation preference of Treasury-owned senior preferred stock is increased. As of June 30, 2012, Treasury reported investments of $187 billion in senior preferred stock.

- **HFA Initiative** In addition, Treasury implemented the HFA Initiative with two programs to support state and local HFAs. Through those programs, Treasury purchased securities from Fannie Mae and Freddie Mac backed by state and local HFA bonds (New Issue Bond Program) and participation interests in liquidity facilities provided to the HFAs by Fannie Mae and Freddie Mac (Temporary Credit and Liquidity Program). As of June 30, 2012, Treasury owns $15.3 billion of Fannie Mae and Freddie Mac securities supporting the New Issue Bond Program and $7.4 billion participation interest in the Temporary Credit and Liquidity Program.

- **Capital Magnet Fund** The act also authorized a new program for CDFI Fund to administer—the Capital Magnet Fund (CMF). It is intended to create a new source of grants for both rental and for-sale housing, as well as for community and economic development. The program is supposed to increase the flow of capital to organizations that will engage in housing-related investments. The CMF is a competitive grant program expected to attract private capital. There are two types of eligible grantees under the fund: (1) CDFIs that have been certified by CDFI Fund and (2) nonprofit organizations having as one of their principal purposes the development or management of affordable housing. The eligible grant activities and entities eligible to receive grants through the CMF represent a significant expansion for CDFI Fund's core programs. The CMF was funded $80 million through appropriation in fiscal year 2010 for its inaugural award round. Since then, CDFI Fund has not requested to fund the CMF. Under HERA, it was intended that the CMF would be financed through appropriation and transfers from Fannie Mae and Freddie which has not occurred due to the financial condition of the two entities.

Recovery Act

The purpose of the Recovery Act was to provide relief during the current economic downturn by expanding tax, bond, and cash assistance to segments of the economy most affected. Treasury is responsible for overseeing an estimated $150 billion provided through tax relief and Recovery Act funding. An estimated $22 billion is funding administered by Departmental Offices through two tax credit exchange programs that provide payments in lieu of tax credits for specified energy properties and payments to the states in lieu of tax credits for rehabilitation and development of low-income housing projects.

Domestic Assistance

Treasury provides assistance to promote economic growth and raise the standard of living in distressed communities in the U.S. by increasing the availability of business capital and financial services. CDFI Fund, for example, promotes access to capital and local economic growth by (1) directly investing in, supporting, and training CDFIs that provide loans, investments, financial services, and technical assistance to underserved populations and communities; (2) providing incentives to banks to invest in their communities and in other CDFIs; and (3) providing financial and other assistance to Native CDFIs and other Native entities proposing to become or create Native CDFIs through its Native Initiatives. The New Markets Tax Credit program provides investors with a tax credit for investing in communities that are economically distressed or consist of low-income populations. CDFI Fund is authorized to allocate tax credit authority under the program to Community Development Entities, which manage the program's investments in low-income community development projects. In return for a tax credit, investors supply capital to Community Development Entities.

CDFI Fund's activities have been affected by recent economic events, resulting in significant funding increases and new program initiatives in fiscal years 2009 through 2012. Funding for the competitive grant programs doubled in fiscal year 2009, with a $100 million increase provided through the Recovery Act. CDFI Fund's programs were supported in fiscal years 2011 and 2012 with funding levels of $227 million and $221 million, respectively. The CMF, a program discussed above, received $80 million for fiscal year 2010 for its inaugural funding round which was awarded in the beginning of fiscal year 2011. The New Markets Tax Credit program was also expanded, with additional allocation authority provided through the Recovery Act that increased the 2008 and 2009 allocation rounds to $5 billion each. The program was supported at this same level in fiscal year 2010. In fiscal year 2011, the program received $3.5 billion of allocation authority. Since the program's inception in 2000, CDFI Fund has awarded $33 billion of tax credit allocations to Community Development Entities.

The Small Business Jobs Act of 2010 authorized Treasury to guarantee the full amounts of notes and bonds issued by CDFIs that make investments in eligible community and economic development. Guarantees in total may not exceed $1 billion in any fiscal year and are available through September 30, 2014. As administrator, CDFI Fund was required to establish the program's regulations by September 27, 2011, 1 year after the law's enactment date, and implement the program by September 27, 2012. Additionally, the act appropriated $13.5 million to cover CDFI Fund's costs to implement and administer a bond guarantee program. CDFI Fund announced the CDFI Bond Guarantee Program in fiscal year 2011, but did not meet the mandated deadline to establish program regulations. Nonetheless, CDFI Fund expects to stand up this program by the statutory deadline of September 27, 2012. Another key component of the CDFI Bond Guarantee Program is the financing vehicle used by CDFIs issuing bonds and notes that are 100-percent guaranteed by the federal government. Consistent with federal credit policy contained in the OMB's Circular No. A-129, the Federal Financing Bank will purchase the CDFIs' 100-percent guaranteed issues.

The fiscal year 2013 budget proposes to fund CDFI Fund grant programs at its present level of $221 million. Of this amount, $155 million is proposed to be used to support core programs such as the CDFI and Native American CDFI Assistance programs and the Bank Enterprise Award Program. Also included in the fiscal year 2013 proposed amount is funding for two community development initiatives, the Bank On USA and the Healthy Food Financing Initiative, introduced in fiscal year 2012. The Bank On USA is an initiative, authorized in Section 1204 of Dodd-Frank, intended to provide grants, innovation awards, and technical assistance to CDFIs that provide affordable financial services and consumer credit to unbanked and under-banked individuals. This initiative did not receive funding in fiscal year 2012. However, CDFI Fund requested $20 million to finance the program in fiscal year 2013. The Healthy Food Financing Initiative is a joint project with the Department of Agriculture and the Department of Health and Human Services that provides access to nutritious foods for those living in underserved urban and rural communities. The initiative's purpose is to eliminate food deserts in both urban and rural communities. Proposed funding for this initiative is $25 million for fiscal year 2013, a $3 million increase over the fiscal year 2012 appropriation.

The fiscal 2013 budget also proposes to increase CDFI Fund's allocation authority to $7 billion for the New Markets Tax Credit program in fiscal year 2013. Of this amount, $250 million is proposed to be used to attract investments that will support the Healthy Food Financing Initiative.

International Assistance

A prosperous world economy serves the U.S. in many ways, including creating markets for U.S. goods and services and promoting stability and cooperation among nations. Treasury focuses on preventing crises and minimizing the impact of those that occur. International financial institutions, such as the International Monetary Fund and the multilateral development banks, including the World Bank, play a key role in enabling global economic growth and stability. Recent focus has been to resolve and prevent further spread of the financial crisis worldwide.

The Office of International Affairs oversees U.S. interests in international financial institutions. The U.S. participates in these institutions to support poverty reduction, private sector development, the transition to market economies, and sustainable economic growth and development; and thereby to advance U.S. economic, political, and commercial interests abroad. Treasury has the responsibility for ensuring that these institutions appropriately use the resources the U.S. contributes, and for this reason systematically reviews how these institutions use the money the U.S. government invested in them. Improving the effectiveness of the multilateral development banks has been a high priority for the administration. Accordingly, Treasury has been pursuing a reform agenda that emphasizes raising living standards and reducing poverty; measuring the results of U.S. contributions; and strengthening efforts to stimulate private-sector investment, promote good government and the rule of law, and fight corruption.

Exchange Stabilization Fund

The Gold Reserve Act of 1934 established the Exchange Stabilization Fund, a fund to be operated by the Secretary of the Treasury, with the approval of the President. The act authorized the Exchange Stabilization Fund to use its assets to deal in gold and foreign exchange to stabilize the exchange value of the dollar. The fund is used to implement U.S. international monetary and financial policy, including exchange market intervention policy. The fund mainly consists of three types of assets: U.S. government securities, foreign currency assets, and Special Drawing Rights.

The Exchange Stabilization Fund investment guidelines require that to ensure the highest degree of confidence in the underlying securities, the fund's investments are to be limited to claims on respective central banks, the Bank for International Settlements, and sovereign governments and their agencies.[3] The Exchange Stabilization Fund's foreign currency holdings are to be invested so as to ensure that adequate liquidity is maintained to meet anticipated intervention financing needs. Investment maturities are to be timed such that substantial funds come available on a regular basis to

---

[3] The Bank for International Settlements is an international central bank whose mission is to serve central banks in their pursuit of monetary and financial stability and to foster international cooperation in those areas.

meet potential intervention financing needs. In addition, the investment objective of fund's portfolio is to seek a rate of return on each of its currency components that is as high as possible over a full interest rate cycle.

Office of Technical Assistance

The Office of Technical Assistance provides technical assistance to developing and/or transitional countries to help strengthen their financial management capacities as authorized under section 129 of the Foreign Assistance Act of 1961, as amended. The office focuses on the following five core development program areas: (1) budget and financial accountability, (2) government debt issuance and management, (3) banking and finance services, (4) revenue advisory, and (5) economics crimes. Treasury provides on-site resident advisors, as well as temporary advisors, to work with foreign government finance ministries and foreign central banks in managing public financial resources. The office's staff also monitors and evaluates projects in each developing and transitional country selected to receive assistance under one or more of Treasury's five core development areas.

Committee on Foreign Investment in the U.S.

The Committee on Foreign Investment in the U.S. was delegated the presidential function, authorized by section 721 of the Defense Production Act of 1950, to investigate the merger or acquisition of U.S. companies by foreign persons for national security implications. The Secretary of the Treasury chairs the committee, and the Office of International Affairs manages this function on the Secretary's behalf. The committee is required to annually report on (1) whether there is credible evidence of a coordinated strategy by one or more countries or companies to acquire U.S. companies involved in research, development, or production of critical technologies for which the U.S. is a leading producer; and (2) whether there are industrial espionage activities directed or directly assisted by foreign governments against private U.S. companies aimed at obtaining commercial secrets related to critical technologies.

Potential Integrity Risks

We believe that integrity risks for domestic and international assistance programs include the potential (1) unauthorized release of sensitive or classified data; (2) falsification of applications or statements; (3) misuse or mismanagement of federal funds, including irregularities in the award of contracts and misallocation of grant proceeds, payments in lieu of tax credits, or federal tax credits; and (4) failure by assisted entities to deliver on promised services. Of particular concern would be contracts that may be let, or grants, or tax credits, or cash payments in lieu of tax credits that may be awarded, without following standard operating procedures that include appropriate monitoring of funded activities. In addition, we recognize program risks could exist that include the failure to promote economic growth within financially underserved areas of the U.S. or to foster economic stability in other nations. There may also be a corresponding loss of credibility with taxpayers in this country or a loss of U.S. credibility on an international level if these Treasury programs do not function as intended.

In-Progress and Planned Fiscal Year 2013 Projects

Oversight of Programs Authorized by HERA (In-Progress)

The overall objective of our audit oversight of HERA programs is to assess Treasury's use of its authorities under the act. We identified distinct and separate areas of concern that we plan to report on in the fiscal year 2013.

Senior Preferred Stock Purchase Agreements (In-Progress)

We plan to assess Treasury's process for providing solvency to Fannie Mae and Freddie Mac through the purchases of senior preferred stock of the entities. Specifically, we plan to assess Treasury's (1) determinations and considerations required under the act for entering into the agreements to purchases stock, (2) funding decisions, (3) monitoring the compliance with the agreements, and (4) rationale for including dividend and commitment fee requirements in the agreements. Audit work for this project began in fiscal year 2011 and is still ongoing. Given the size of Treasury's investment in Fannie Mae and Freddie Mac and Treasury's continued support of them, we plan future work in this area to evaluate Treasury's monitoring of its investment and the housing market.

HFA Initiative (In-Progress)

We plan to determine whether the two components of the HFA Initiative, the New Issue Bond Program and Temporary Credit Liquidity Program, are being administered consistent with Treasury's authority. Specifically, we plan to assess Treasury's process for (1) monitoring the performance of the financial agents and (2) whether the HFA Initiative is meeting its stated program objectives. Since the HFA Initiative has been extended through 2015, we plan to evaluate Treasury's continued monitoring of housing market indicators for assessing the health of HFAs participating in the HFA initiative.

CDFI Fund Administration of the Capital Magnet Fund

We plan to determine whether CDFI Fund established controls for awarding and administering CMF grant activities. Specifically, we plan to assess CDFI Fund's processes to (1) review whether funds were properly and timely awarded to eligible recipients and (2) ensure awardees' compliance with program requirements to include leveraging award dollars that will provide a dedicated source of funding.

Oversight of Recovery Act Programs

The overall objective of our audit oversight of Treasury's Recovery Act programs is to evaluate management's accountability, control, and oversight of the Department's non-IRS funds and provide recommendations for improving operations and preventing fraud, waste, and abuse with respect to those funds. Through a series of audits, described below, we will determine whether Treasury timely and effectively implemented program activities for awarding Recovery Act funding.

Payments in Lieu of Tax Credits for Specified Energy Properties (Ongoing)

We plan to determine whether Treasury is timely and effectively implementing activities for awarding and monitoring payments in lieu of tax credits for specified energy properties under the Recovery Act. We plan to assess the eligibility of award recipients and whether recipients are in compliance with award requirements. Audit work for this project began in April 2009 and will continue in fiscal year 2013.

Payments to States for Low-Income Housing Projects in Lieu of Low-Income Housing Credits (Ongoing)

We plan to determine whether Treasury is timely and effectively implementing activities for awarding and monitoring payments to the states in lieu of tax credits for low-income housing under the Recovery Act. We will assess (1) the eligibility of potential grant applicants at both the state and subaward level, (2) subawardees' compliance with award requirements, and (3) internal control procedures to ensure subawardees do not receive both tax credits and payments. Audit work for this project began in April 2009 and will continue in fiscal year 2013. We will coordinate with TIGTA to ensure subawardees are not receiving both Recovery Act funds and low-income housing credits for the same properties.

CDFI Fund Administration of Recovery Act Funds (Ongoing)

We plan to determine whether CDFI Fund timely and effectively awarded the additional $100 million in funding provided under the Recovery Act for grant program activities. We plan to (1) assess eligibility of potential award recipients, (2) evaluate effectiveness of internal control over grant awards, and (3) ensure recipient compliance with award requirements. Audit work for this project began in April 2009 and is being performed in phases. We have completed the first phase, in which we assessed the eligibility of potential award recipients. As discussed in our report, *Recovery Act: The Community Development Financial Institutions Fund Needs to Improve Its Process for Awarding Assistance to Applicants,* (OIG-11-079; July 8, 2011), we found that in awarding Recovery Act funds, CDFI Fund did not comply with certain statutory requirements of the Recovery Act We plan to complete our work on the remaining phases in fiscal year 2013.

Tax Credits Taken for Specified Energy Properties

We plan to coordinate with TIGTA to determine whether Treasury established and maintained internal control procedures to prevent recipients from improperly receiving both tax credits and Recovery Act payments for the same specified energy properties.

Corrective Action Verification on CDFI Fund Recovery Act Report

We plan to determine whether CDFI Fund management took corrective action responsive to our recommendations in audit report, *Recovery Act: The Community Development Financial Institutions Fund Needs to Improve Its Process for Awarding Assistance to Applicants,* (OIG-11-079; July 8, 2011).

New Markets Tax Credit Program Award Process and Compliance Monitoring (In-Progress)

We plan to assess the New Markets Tax Credit program's (1) application and tax credit allocation process, (2) assessment of the eligibility of potential award recipients, (3) internal control over and monitoring of program awards, and (4) process for ensuring recipient compliance with tax credit allocation agreements. Audit work for this project began in February 2010 with focus on the effectiveness of CDFI Fund's allocation of the increased authority provided by the Recovery Act. We completed the award phase of this project in fiscal year 2012 and plan to conclude on the compliance monitoring phase in fiscal year 2013. As part of this audit, we will follow up on issues identified in GAO's 2010 report, *New Markets Tax Credit: The Credit Helps Fund a Variety of Projects in Low-Income Communities, but Could Be Simplified,* (GAO-10-334; Jan. 29, 2010).

Other Planned Fiscal Year 2013 Projects

CDFI Fund Implementation and Administration of the Healthy Foods Financing Initiative

We plan to determine whether CDFI Fund implemented program activities for carrying out its responsibility to administer the Healthy Food Financing Initiative. Specifically, we plan to (1) determine whether CDFI Fund awarded funds and New Market Tax Credit allocations to eligible recipients in accordance with applicable laws and regulations; (2) ensure that CDFI Fund established and maintained proper internal control procedures and oversight over grants and tax credit allocations for ensuring that program recipients meet eligibility requirements and properly comply with award agreements; and (3) assess CDFI Fund's process for measuring the Healthy Food Financing Initiative's performance/outcomes to ensure that the program's objectives achieve its intended purposes.

Bond Guarantee Program

We plan to determine whether CDFI Fund implemented program activities to carry out its responsibility to administer the Bond Guarantee Program required by the Small Business Jobs Act of 2010.

CDFI Fund's Analysis of Eligibility Requirements Based on 2006-2010 Census Data

CDFI fund is in the process of analyzing the 2006-2010 American Community Survey Census Bureau data to update eligible geographic areas for its programs based on poverty and income data.

We plan to assess the progress of CDFI Fund's analysis.

Single Audits

We plan to perform quality control reviews to determine whether audits obtained by CDFIs were performed in accordance with the Single Audit requirements and applicable professional standards and may be relied upon for ensuring accountability of CDFI Fund awards. Additionally, we will assess CDFI Fund's process for (1) reviewing Single Audit reports, (2) determining the impact any findings may have on financial assistance received from CDFI Fund, and (3) ensuring Single Audit findings are resolved.

Survey of the Committee on Foreign Investment in the U.S.

We plan to determine how Treasury supports the Committee on Foreign Investment in the U.S. in identifying and addressing national security concerns arising from covered transactions with foreign investors. We will also determine whether measures have been implemented to identify foreign investors who have not filed with the committee.

Projects Under Consideration for Future Fiscal Years

CDFI Fund Implementation and Administration of the Bank on USA Initiative

We plan to determine whether CDFI Fund implemented program activities for carrying out its responsibility to implement and administer the Bank on USA Initiative if funded in fiscal year 2013. Specific subject areas include (1) determining whether CDFI Fund implemented the Bank of USA Initiative for awarding grants to eligible applicants for eligible activities; (2) ensuring that CDFI Fund established and maintained proper internal control procedures and oversight over grants ensuring that program recipients meet eligibility requirements and properly comply with award agreements; and (3) assessing CDFI Fund's process for measuring the Bank of USA Initiative's performance/outcomes to ensure that the program objectives are achieved.

Bank Enterprise Awards

We plan to assess CDFI Fund's process for awarding and monitoring awards made through the Bank Enterprise Awards Program. Specifically, we plan to (1) determine whether CDFI Fund awarded the appropriated funds to eligible recipients based on qualified activities in accordance with applicable laws and regulations; (2) ensure that CDFI Fund established and maintained proper internal control procedures and oversight over the program's awards to include follow up on recommendations provided in our prior audit report, *Awards to One United Bank Were Consistent With Requirements But Certain Aspects of CDFI Fund Program Administration Need to Be Revisited,* (OIG-11-091; Aug. 3, 2011); and (3) assess CDFI Fund's process for measuring the program's performance/outcomes to ensure that the program objectives are achieved.

CDFI Fund's Tracking of Awardees Across Multiple Assistance Programs

We plan to assess CDFI Fund's coordination for tracking awardees receiving awards under multiple programs to ensure funds are used appropriately in targeted markets.

Survey of Treasury's Participation in the International Monetary Fund

We plan to gain an understanding of Treasury's role for promoting U.S. policy with respect to the International Monetary Fund.

Multilateral Development Banks

We plan to gain an understanding of Treasury's process for ensuring U.S. policy is carried out though the multilateral development banks. As part of this project, we plan to assess Treasury's participation and role with respect to global initiatives.

Treasury's Global Agriculture and Food Security Program

We plan to gain an understanding of Treasury's role in the Global Agriculture and Food Security Program, including how funds are granted in accordance with applicable guidance and collectively how funds are used to improve impoverished nations.

Debt Relief Programs

We plan to gain an understanding of Treasury's role in debt reduction programs with nations indebted to the U.S. and its process for ensuring indebted nations meet eligibility requirements for relief.

Office of Technical Assistance Programs

We plan to assess Treasury's Office of Technical Assistance administration of programs established to provide technical assistance to foreign governments and foreign central banks in developing transitional countries. As part of this audit, we plan to evaluate the office's process for selecting central governments and banks for receiving assistance under any of the office's five technical assistance programs, as well as how the office selects technical experts. We also plan to assess the office's monitoring of its program projects.

Treaties and International Agreements

We plan to gain an understanding of treaties and international agreements with foreign governments Treasury entered into on behalf of the U.S. government and Treasury's coordination and/or consultation with the Department of State.

Transfer of Funds Under the Foreign Assistance Act of 1961

The U.S. Agency for International Development transferred $66.6 million to Treasury in fiscal year 2010 for contributions to the Global Agriculture and Food Security Program Trust Fund. The agency transferred another $125 million in fiscal year 2011 funds to Treasury for contributions to the Haiti Reconstruction Fund. Under memoranda of understanding between the U.S. Agency for International Development and Treasury, we are responsible for performing periodic program and financial audits of the use of the transferred funds, and the cost of the audits may be paid from transferred funds.

We plan to determine whether Treasury administered the transferred funds in accordance with applicable laws.

Exchange Stabilization Fund Investment Portfolio

We plan to (1) gain an understanding of the policy for the Exchange Stabilization Fund's investments in securities and foreign currency denominated assets, (2) gain an understanding of the factors considered in implementing the investment policy, and (3) determine whether the Fund complied with policy in its purchases, management, and sales of investments and foreign currency denominated assets.

SBLF and SSBCI Operations

Issue Area Discussion

The Small Business Jobs Act of 2010, which was signed into law on September 27, 2010, established two programs, SBLF and SSBCI. The act also created within OIG the Office of SBLF Program Oversight. Under Section 4107(a) of the act, the Special Deputy Inspector General for SBLF Program Oversight is responsible for audit and investigations related to SBLF and SSBCI programs and must report at least twice a year to the Secretary of the Treasury and the Congress on the results of oversight activities involving the SBLF program. The Special Deputy is also responsible for identifying instances of intentional or reckless misuse of SSBCI funds.

SBLF Operations

The SBLF program was created to provide capital to small banks, with incentives for those banks to increase small business lending. Generally, SBLF was open only to insured depository institutions with under $10 billion in assets as well as bank holding companies or savings and loan holding companies, each with aggregate assets of under $10 billion. Entities that met the asset-size requirement were eligible to participate in the program if they were not on FDIC's "problem list" or had not been removed from that list in the 90 days previous to application. SBLF also provided an option for community banks to refinance preferred stock issued to Treasury through the TARP Capital Purchase Plan or the Community Development Capital Initiative if the banks had not missed more than one dividend payment under either of these two programs. Under the SBLF program, banks may not make loans to entities with over $50 million in revenues or in original amounts over $10 million. Loans must also meet underwriting standards established by the banks' primary banking regulators.

Treasury disbursed more than $4 billion to 332 financial institutions across the country, of which 137 were institutions that used their SBLF investment to refinance securities issued under TARP. The 137 TARP banks received two-thirds of the $4 billion invested in participating banks. Institutions receiving investments under the SBLF program are expected to pay dividends to Treasury at rates that will decrease as the amount of their qualified small business lending increases. In July 2012, Treasury reported that institutions participating in SBLF had increased their small business lending by $5.2 billion over baseline levels as of March 31, 2012. Moreover, Treasury reported that 84 percent of the SBLF participants had achieved small business lending increases, and 69 percent had increased their small business lending by 10 percent or more.

Potential Weaknesses Particular to SBLF

SBLF has a similar structure to TARP, and the comparison has given rise to concerns about Treasury's approach to funding banks. Various parties have alleged, in particular, that SBLF provides a means for banks to exit cheaply from TARP. The overall health and viability of the participating institutions is also of significant interest, and the program has been viewed as a means to support otherwise failing smaller banks. Our planned audits will look closely at the ability of banks to repay Treasury's investment and whether Treasury consistently applied its evaluation criteria in approving applicants for the SBLF program. We will also determine whether SBLF participants are accurately reporting their small business lending activity, which is used by Treasury to establish dividend rates and measure program impact.

Treasury will face many challenges in ensuring that the SBLF program meets its intended objective of increasing lending to small businesses, and measuring program performance. Under the terms of the authorizing legislation, the SBLF funds are intended to stimulate lending to small businesses, but participating institutions are under no obligation to increase their small business lending activity. Once SBLF funds are disbursed and become comingled with other funds of the participating institutions, it will be difficult to track how the funds are spent. Participants are also not required to report how they use Treasury's investments. Additionally, Treasury is reliant on unverified information reported by participating institutions on their small business lending activity to measure performance and to make dividend rate adjustments.

Finally, dividend payments, which constitute Treasury's sole source of revenue from the SBLF program, are essentially optional, as they are non-cumulative and non-accruing. Treasury has indicated that when dividend payments are missed, it will take additional measures ranging from requiring an explanation for the missed payment to electing directors to an institution's board of directors. However, these measures may be ineffective if the institution's regulator has restricted it from making dividend payments. Institutions are also under no obligation to pay off previously missed payments.

In-Progress and Planned Fiscal Year 2013 Projects

Quarterly Adjusted SBLF Dividend Rates for the Third Quarter of 2012

We plan to determine the accuracy of small business lending activity for the third quarter of 2012 reported by SBLF participants for dividend rate adjustments.

Use of SBLF Funds by Participating Institutions

We plan to determine (1) how institutions participating in the SBLF program have used program funds, (2) the extent to which increases in small business lending occurred prior to institutions entering the program, (3) the number and types of small businesses receiving loan assistance and (4) the extent to which businesses were assisted that would not otherwise have secured funding.

Quarterly Adjusted SBLF Dividend Rates for the Fourth Quarter of 2012

We plan to determine the accuracy of small business lending activity for the fourth quarter of 2012 reported by SBLF participants for dividend rate adjustments.

Treasury's Handling of Missed Dividend Payments and Requests for Restructuring Investments

We plan to determine whether (1) Treasury is taking appropriate action to collect missed dividend payments, and (2) restructurings of SBLF investments are justified and conducted in a manner that minimizes risk to the federal government.

Projects Under Consideration for Future Fiscal Years

Use of SBLF Investments by Community Development Loan Funds

We plan to determine whether Community Development Loan Funds participating in SBLF (1) obtained sufficient subsidized capital needed for small business lending and repayment of Treasury's investment, (2) achieved the amount of leverage expected with the SBLF capital provided them, and (3) used all of the capital leveraged to increase small business lending.

Effectiveness of the SBLF in Increasing Lending to Small Businesses and Creating Jobs

We plan to determine (1) the number, types, and sizes of small businesses receiving loan assistance, (2) the number of jobs created as a result of loans made to small businesses, and (3) whether loans are being made to businesses that would not otherwise have secured financial assistance from commercial lenders.

SSBCI Operations

SSBCI is a $1.5 billion initiative that provides participating states, territories, and eligible municipalities with funding to support state programs that provide lending to, and investment in, small businesses. SSBCI builds on new and existing models for state small business programs, including those that finance loan loss reserves and provide loan insurance, loan guaranties, venture capital funds, and collateral support. As of June 30, 2012, Treasury had awarded 54 states, territories, and municipalities $1.4 billion in SSBCI funding. States must provide plans for using their funding allocations to Treasury for review and approval and report quarterly and annually on results. Another key feature is that participating states receive their allocations in three increments. As of June 30, 2012, Treasury had disbursed $524 million of the funds awarded under the program. Treasury may withhold a successive increment to a state pending the results of an audit by our office.

Potential Weaknesses Particular to SSBCI

Primary oversight of the use of SSBCI funds is the responsibility of each participating state. The states are required to provide Treasury with quarterly assurances that their programs approved for SSBCI funding are in compliance with program requirements. However, Treasury will face challenges in holding states accountable for the proper use of funds as it has not set minimum requirements for state oversight activities. While Treasury issued SSBCI National Standards in May 2012 outlining a framework for states to use in designing and implementing an oversight system for SSBCI funds, implementation of the framework is optional. As a result, Treasury cannot be assured that participating states are engaging in the necessary oversight activities to ensure that program requirements are being met. Treasury will also have difficulty holding states accountable should OIG find that a state has intentionally or recklessly misused funds. Finally, oversight of state programs will be difficult as each state can have multiple programs that differ in design and complexity.

In-Progress and Planned Fiscal Year 2013 Projects

SSBCI On-Site Reviews (Ongoing)

We have several ongoing and planned reviews of selected lenders and other institutions funded by participating states to identify intentional or reckless misuse of SSBCI program funds.

Projects Under Consideration for Future Fiscal Years

SSBCI On-Site Reviews

We will continue to conduct on-site reviews of participating states requesting additional tranches of funding to identify any intentional or reckless misuse of funds prior to Treasury's disbursement of a state's full allocation.

Effectiveness of SSBCI in Increasing Access to Capital for Small Businesses

We plan to determine (1) the number and types of small businesses provided access to capital assistance, (2) the number of jobs created as a result of loans made to small businesses, and (3) whether loans are being made to businesses that would not otherwise have secured funding.

Treasury's Recoupment of Misused SSBCI Funds and Handling of Compliance Issues

We plan to determine whether Treasury is taking appropriate action to (1) collect funds that OIG has identified as intentionally or recklessly misused and (2) ensure that compliance issues identified by OIG audits have been addressed.

Gulf Coast Restoration Trust Fund Oversight

Issue Area Discussion

Mandate

The Gulf Coast Restoration Trust Fund was established by the Restore Act of Public Law 112-141. The act requires the Secretary of the Treasury to deposit in the trust fund 80 percent of all administrative and civil penalties paid by responsible parties pursuant to a court order, negotiated settlement, or other instrument in accordance with the Federal Water Pollution Control Act in connection with the explosion on, and sinking of, the mobile offshore drilling unit Deepwater Horizon. The trust fund is to be available (1) for expenditure to restore the Gulf Coast region from the Deepwater Horizon oil spill for undertaking projects and programs to restore and protect the natural resources, ecosystems, fisheries, marine and wildlife habitats, beaches, coastal wetlands, and economy of that region; and (2) solely to the Gulf Coast states of Alabama, Florida, Louisiana, Mississippi, and Texas to restore the ecosystems and economy of the Gulf Coast region.

Of the total amount made available for disbursement from the trust fund during any fiscal year,

- 35 percent shall be available to the Gulf Coast states, in equal shares, for expenditure for ecological and economic restoration of the Gulf Coast region,

- 30 percent shall be disbursed to the Gulf Coast Ecosystem Restoration Council pursuant to the council's approval of its comprehensive plan to undertake projects and programs using the best available science that would restore and protect the natural resources, ecosystems, fisheries, marine and wildlife habitats, beaches, coastal wetlands, and economy of the Gulf Coast region;

- 30 percent shall be disbursed to the Gulf Coast Ecosystem Restoration Council for allocation to the Gulf Coast states for eligible oil spill restoration activities, pursuant to the council's approval of the state's plan to improve the ecosystems or economy of the Gulf Coast region, using a regulatory formula;

- 2.5 percent shall be allocated to the National Oceanic and Atmospheric Administration for its Gulf Coast Ecosystem Restoration Science, Observation, Monitoring, and Technology Program. This program must be established by January 2013 by the Administrator of the National Oceanic and Atmospheric Administration to carry out research, observation, and monitoring to support, to the maximum extent practicable, the long-term sustainability of the ecosystem, fish stocks, fish habitat, and the recreational, commercial, and charter fishing industry in the Gulf of Mexico; and

- 2.5 percent shall be made available to the Gulf Coast states, in equal shares, exclusively for competitive grant awards to nongovernmental entities and consortia in the Gulf Coast region, including public and private institutions of higher education, to establish centers for excellence to conduct research only on the Gulf Coast region.

Treasury's authority to administer the Gulf Coast Restoration Trust Fund terminates on the date all amounts are expended from the trust fund.

The Restore Act provides Treasury with remedies for a state's noncompliance with the conditions of the trust fund; Treasury may cut off funding to a state until the state either repays the trust fund or the state substitutes an ineligible activity with an eligible activity.

The act provides Treasury OIG jurisdictional oversight authority to conduct, supervise, and coordinate audits and investigations of projects, programs, and activities funded under the act and the amendments made to the act. The act does not fund Treasury OIG's oversight.

Program Responsibilities

Treasury is required to establish procedures for depositing amounts in and expending amounts from the Gulf Coast Restoration Trust Fund by January 2013, including procedures for (1) assessing whether a trust fund expenditure by a Gulf Coast state for a program or activity achieves compliance with the conditions of the trust fund; (2) auditing requirements to ensure that amounts in the trust fund are expended as intended; and (3) identification and allocation of funds available to the Secretary of the Treasury necessary to pay administrative expenses directly attributable to the management of the trust fund. Treasury OIG's early involvement in assessing the effectiveness of Treasury's process to establish procedures is essential to ensuring amounts in the trust fund are expended as intended.

Planned Fiscal Year 2013 Projects

Review of the Establishment and Effectiveness of Treasury's Administration of the Gulf Coast Restoration Trust Fund

We plan to assess Treasury's process to establish procedures for depositing amounts in and expending amounts from the Gulf Coast Restoration Trust Fund.

Review of States Administration of Gulf Coast Restoration Trust Fund Activities

We plan to determine whether states are distributing and administering Gulf Coast Restoration Trust funds to eligible parties in an appropriate manner.

Review of Treasury's Oversight of Gulf Coast Restoration Trust Fund Programs Administered by the Gulf Coast Ecosystem Restoration Council and National Oceanic and Atmospheric Administration

We plan to determine, in coordination with other federal, state, and local accountability organizations, whether an appropriate level of oversight is being exercised for Gulf Coast Restoration Trust Fund programs administered by the Gulf Coast Ecosystem Restoration Council and the National Oceanic and Atmospheric Administration.

Appendix A: Office of Audit
Fiscal Year 2013 Resource Allocation

Our planned OIG staff resource utilization by the three priority areas for fiscal year 2013 is shown in the following table:

Audit Priority	Percentage of Planned Audit Resources
Audit products mandated by law	32
Work requested by Congress or externally driven	10
Self-directed work in Treasury's highest-risk areas	58
Total	**100**

Our planned OIG audit staff resource allocation by OIG Issue Area is shown in the following table:

OIG Issue Area	Percentage of Planned Audit Resources
Treasury general management and infrastructure support:	
Financial management	8
Information security	9
General management	6
Terrorist financing, money laundering, and foreign assets control	12
Government-wide financial services and debt management	10
Safety, soundness, and accessibility of financial services	20
Revenue collections and industry regulation	3
Bill and coin manufacturing, marketing, and distribution operations	6
Domestic and international assistance programs	12
Small Business Lending Fund and State Small Business Credit Initiative Operations	12
Gulf Coast Restoration Trust Fund Oversight	2
Total	**100**

Appendix A: Office of Audit Fiscal Year 2013 Resource Allocation

The table below shows planned OIG audit staff allocation by Treasury headquarters operational component and bureau:

Treasury Component	Percentage of Planned Audit Resources
Departmental Offices:	
Domestic Finance	9
Office of the Assistant Secretary for Management and Chief Financial Officer	8
Small Business Lending Fund	6
State Small Business Credit Initiative	6
Community Development Financial Institutions Fund	5
Office of the Chief Information Officer	4
Office of Foreign Assets Control	4
Office of Terrorism and Financial Intelligence	2
Office of Financial Research	2
Gulf Coast Restoration Trust Fund	2
Treasury Executive of Asset Forfeiture	1
International Affairs	0
Federal Financing Bank	0
Federal Insurance Office	0
Office of Technical Assistance	0
Bureaus:	
Office of the Comptroller of the Currency	22
Bureau of the Fiscal Service	9
Financial Crimes Enforcement Network	7
Mint	6
Bureau of Engraving and Printing	4
Alcohol and Tobacco Tax and Trade Bureau	3
Total	**100**

Appendix B: Index of In-Progress and Planned Fiscal Year 2013 Audits by Issue Area

Appendix B: Index of In-Progress and Planned Fiscal Year 2013 Audits by Issue Area

Appendix B: Index of In-Progress and Planned Fiscal Year 2013 Audits by Issue Area

Appendix C: Index of In-Progress and Planned Fiscal Year 2013 Audits by Bureau/Office

Multi Bureau

Departmental Offices

Appendix C: Index of In-Progress and Planned Fiscal Year 2013 Audits by Bureau/Office

Appendix C: Index of In-Progress and Planned Fiscal Year 2013 Audits by Bureau/Office

Appendix D: Index of Projects Under Consideration for Future Fiscal Years

Appendix D: Index of Projects Under Consideration for Future Fiscal Years

Appendix D: Index of Projects Under Consideration for Future Fiscal Years

Appendix D: Index of Projects Under Consideration for Future Fiscal Years

Abbreviations

BEN	Bureau of Engraving and Printing's Enterprise Network System
BEP	Bureau of Engraving and Printing
BFS	Bureau of the Fiscal Service
BPD	Bureau of the Public Debt
BSA	Bank Secrecy Act
CDFI	Community Development Financial Institutions
CHIPRA	Children's Health Insurance Program Reauthorization Act of 2009
CMF	Capital Magnet Fund
Dodd-Frank	Dodd-Frank Wall Street Reform and Consumer Protection Act
E.O.	Executive Order
FDIC	Federal Deposit Insurance Corporation
FinCEN	Financial Crimes Enforcement Network
FISMA	Federal Information Security Management Act
FMS	Financial Management Service
FRB	Board of Governors of the Federal Reserve System
GAO	Government Accountability Office
HERA	Housing and Economic Recovery Act of 2008
HFA	Housing Finance Agencies
IRS	Internal Revenue Service
IT	information technology
OCC	Office of the Comptroller of the Currency
OFAC	Office of Foreign Assets Control
OIG	Office of Inspector General
OMB	Office of Management and Budget
OTS	Office of Thrift Supervision
Plan	Joint Implementation Plan
Recovery Act	American Recovery and Reinvestment Act
Restore Act	Resources and Ecosystems Sustainability, Tourist Opportunities, and Revived Economies of the Gulf Coast States Act of 2012
SBLF	Small Business Lending Fund
SSBCI	State Small Business Credit Initiative
TARP	Troubled Asset Relief Program
TIGTA	Treasury Inspector General for Tax Administration
TNet	Treasury Network
Treasury	Department of the Treasury
TTB	Alcohol and Tobacco Tax and Trade Bureau
XBRL	eXtensible Business Reporting Language

contact us

Headquarters
Office of Inspector General
1500 Pennsylvania Avenue, N.W.
Room 4436
Washington, D.C. 20220
Phone: (202) 622-1090;
Fax: (202) 622-2151

**Office of Small Business Lending
Fund Program Oversight**
1425 New York Avenue, Suite 5041
Washington, D.C. 20220
Phone: (202) 622-1090;
 Fax: (202) 927-5421

Office of Audit
740 15th Street, N.W., Suite 600
Washington, D.C. 20220
Phone: (202) 927-5400;
Fax: (202) 927-5379

Office of Investigations
1425 New York Avenue, Suite 5041
Washington, D.C. 20220
Phone: (202) 927-5260;
Fax: (202) 927-5421

Office of Counsel
740 15th Street, N.W., Suite 510
Washington, D.C. 20220
Phone: (202) 927-0650;
Fax: (202) 927-5418

Office of Management
740 15th Street, N.W., Suite 510
Washington, D.C. 20220
Phone: (202) 927-5200;
Fax: (202) 927-6492

Boston Audit Office
408 Atlantic Avenue, Room 330
Boston, Massachusetts 02110-3350
Phone: (617) 223-8640;
Fax (617) 223-8651

Treasury OIG Hotline
Call Toll Free: 1.800.359.3898

Treasury OIG Web Page

OIG reports and other information are now available via the Internet. The address is
http://www.treasury.gov/about/organizational-structure/ig/Pages/default.aspx